LEAVING THE SUBURBS

A journalistic primer on politics,
climate change, and unsustainable debt

John Ernest Duke

To Pat & Conna,

Conservation
Lives!

Good luck in all
your endeavours.

John E Duke

ISBN-13: 978-0-9600089-0-2

Design and production by Joanne Shwed, Backspace Ink (www.backspaceink.com)

Except for celebrities, the names of the people in these stories have either been changed entirely or first names only may have been used on some occasions.

All maps and photographs created by the author.

Artwork credits:
Chapter 1: Marianne Lecesne / Anne McCallum
Chapter 2: author (map)
Chapter 3 / 4 / 5: Anne McCallum
Chapter 6 / 7 / 8: author

Contents

Prologue: Travels by Bicycle

THIS STORY TOGGLES BETWEEN a past event and the near present moment: a la James Michener style...one of my favorite historical fiction writers. The past event is *real* though, a solo bicycle ride through four major continental watersheds, eleven states, and four counties with so few people, less than two per square mile, that they would be considered "frontier" according to standards established by the US Census Bureau. It forms the framework to keep us moving along on the journey. The story also toggles between the far distant past and an analysis of ecological principles that I now understand through formal education, field research, and the experiences of building a second career. I hope to explain why these ecological principles are important in their application to our modern society. Those fundamental ecological principles require us to make personal decisions that help drive public decisions in how we protect the public welfare for everyone.

Truth be told, everybody has a story. Like the guy who has lived on a ranch in Wyoming all his life and was mauled by a grizzly – twice – and survived - and he *still* thinks they should be protected and that humans should coexist with them. You have a story too. You just haven't told it maybe. This is my story. It's my way to express to you that it is important that you feel empowered by your everyday choices.

I write so that when future generations ask, "Why didn't you do something?" there will be a record that says, "I did." I believe that we are sleep walking as though we are unaware of some of the greatest challenges facing humanity. Previous generations have had some pretty big ones – world wars, pandemics, institutional racism, ethnic genocide to name just a few. Not that some of those issues may still have relevance. But I think that the biggest ones facing us today are climate change and unprecedented debt. And I believe that the two are related.

I have tried to live by the idea of "private sufficiency and public luxury." To me that equates to living below your means, having a savings account, and visiting the best public spaces in your community, your country, or your continent. It means we should demand that public resources be used wisely. It means basic things like clean affordable water should be a right and should never be manipulated for corporate profits. It means we should cherish a free market but never take the public domain for granted – those things that are paid for collectively and that afford us great freedom.

Don't let anyone tell you how rich everybody else is. The median household income in the United States is around $50,000 and 80% of households earn less than $100,000. And saying that we all can be "rich" is the economic equivalent of saying that you can defy gravity. It is the equivalent of saying every high school quarterback can go to the NFL. In fact, less than one tenth of 1% (0.08 percent) ever will. For a great story on this itself I refer you to Steve Levitt and Stephen Dubner's book *Freakonomics*, specifically the chapter entitled "Why Do Drug Dealers Still Live with Their Moms?" After Hurricane Maria devastated Puerto Rico, a volunteer working the *Banco de Alimentos* in the city of Bayamon said, "Even people with money need the food bank because there was no food to buy in the stores." This cold reality highlights the fact that we are all in this together. So we, those of us who are the "ordinary" citizens of the world, collectively are the economic engine just by our sheer numbers. And if everyone can be rich, then we start to generate a false economy whereby we consume the natural resources at a rate the earth cannot sustain. That, to me, is just another way of saying "unsustainable debt."

Personally, I feel a responsibility as though we are the ones in charge now. I won't be so dramatic as to say those challenges threaten our very existence but they at least feel like they threaten our existence *without chaos*. But while I carry this anxiety with me like a heavy piece of luggage, or should I say a loaded down bicycle, I think I have still been able to carve out some fascinating stories here and I hope you enjoy the journey. Thank you for reading. – jd

Glacier National Park

Take the long way home.

I KNOW WHAT IT is like to be a rock star without actually being a rock star. There were complete strangers asking me to pose with them for the camera. It was usually the person's spouse or mom or brother or whoever that snapped the picture with a Canon AE1. I would smile and lean with one leg crossed and my arm resting on their shoulder and for a brief moment it was as though we were best friends.

I had just pedaled halfway up the western slope of the Continental Divide in Glacier National Park on a bicycle. The traffic on the Going-to-the-Sun Road (Sun Road for short) in the summertime was so congested that a curfew had been imposed on bicycles from 10AM to 4PM. Therefore, I was pulled over in The Loop, a parking lot built inside the pocket formed by a hairpin curve, right at about 9:59. I think people had seen bicyclers before but not ones riding a bike loaded down with 30 pounds of gear, and not on a 17-foot wide strip of asphalt hanging on a cliff jammed against a vertical granite wall. Whatever it was, the motorist jumped out of their cars in fascination at my endeavor. It was the 3rd day of July and dripping ice still hung on the north facing sides of the wall, a wall so close you could reach out and touch, as the road cut in and out on a switchback on its way to the pass. The sweet aroma of conifer trees filled the subtle breezy mountain air under a clear blue sky only visible in long, thin slivers between the peaks. The ice on the wall seemed oddly out of place as the warm sun gently beat down on me and a tiny bead of sweat popped out on my forehead. I swear I could feel cool air release from the wall as the frozen water absorbed the day's energy and turned to a flowing liquid. This little part of the continent seemed to be declaring that this was the day, finally *the* day, *the* moment, that spring transitioned into summer this year. The other side of the road from the wall was thin air - a 1000-foot cliff. And it was as though you were a slow moving pin ball bumping through a narrow corridor and hemmed in between rock and guard railings.

I was on summer break from college and was on my way home after visiting relatives who lived on the west coast. Since leaving Everett, Washington, I was now crossing my second mountain range, entering a second time zone, and had traveled nearly 600 miles. An automobile could have easily completed that distance in a day. I had already pedaled for 56 hours and had burned 36,400 calories. My friends thought that I would never make it back in time for fall classes because I would be stopping every few feet to pick up aluminum cans. Before I left, they had drawn on the chalk board in the hallway of the dorm, a stick image sitting on a bicycle, smiling, and tossing a can over his shoulder into a trailer being towed.

I had been harassing them to stop throwing away so much stuff and had started the first recycling program in the dorm. Today recycling has become so main stream that overwhelming peer pressure compels everyone to participate in communities all across the country. There are lively discussions on social media about what and what not to recycle and how it should be done properly. But is anyone buying recycled products? The truth is that we can't recycle our way out of trash. Recycling has now almost become a means to absolve us so-to-speak.[1] At the time of my ride though, I just thought, "How silly can they be? I don't have time for that." Besides, I didn't have a trailer and I didn't have a support vehicle. I was riding alone and all of my possessions were on a rack over the back wheel or in panniers hanging off of it. I had a piece of rope with which to form a centerline for the rainfly. I had a sleeping bag, a backpacking stove, a bottle of liquid fuel that lasted about 8 days, and some food. I had a toothbrush, a bowl, a knife, a spoon, a change of socks and underwear, an extra T-shirt, and a fleece packed away for the cool nights. I wore spandex biking shorts, a T-shirt, a bike helmet, a side mirror attached to my eyeglasses, and flip down sunglasses. Two water bottles were in hangers attached to the bike frame.

But my friends did know me well and they called me "Nature Boy." I was in veterinary school at Auburn University and I had contemplated dropping out many times. A confidante outside of my circle of academics convinced me that I could make an impact in the "big picture" through a public health career so I stuck it on through at least for the time being. During the last week of school during final exams I read a treatise on the implications of the industrial revolution on the carbon cycle. I also had a knack for historical fiction and another time during finals I had read *Gone With The Wind* by Margaret Mitchell for the second time in my life. People stopped by my dorm room and asked incredulously, "Aren't you studying?" I picked up *National Geographic*, *Outdoor Magazine*, and *Popular Science* whenever I had a few extra dollars. I read the newspaper looking for the latest science and environmental reporting like I was digging for gold.

I made my classmates carpool wherever we couldn't walk. The intramural basketball coach asked me why I was so concerned about pollution when cars now had catalytic converters. I said, "It's not CO, its CO *two*." This was long before Al Gore made his crusade and so when people today tell me they don't like a politician, especially a Democrat, telling them what to do I say, "It was *me* who told *Al Gore*." For some reason they don't believe me. It could be that I have never met the man in my life and I certainly didn't know who he was when I was explaining to my classmate what exactly catalytic converters do and don't do.

Caroline, my girlfriend and who was also in my proposed graduating class at Auburn, flew with me to Washington. As we sat in the SeaTac Airport waiting on her return flight to board she asked, "Are you sure that you want to do this?"

"Do what?"

"Ride a bicycle home."

"Come on Caroline. You know I have been planning and training for months."

"OK. Promise you will call home often?"

"Promise."

We had a rocky relationship. She loved me but I think she wanted someone more committed to a real career. Although I never confided in her I just knew that she knew I had other notions than the path I was on. You were supposed to be thankful for the opportunity to have a chance at a lucrative career like medicine or law. And I suppose that I was being irreverent and disrespectful. I didn't want to hurt her feelings at a time like this and so I just smiled and gently held her hand as I kept the thought to myself, "Look Caroline! It is my choice if I do not wish to finish school!"

I estimated that I had a few days to think about it...

CAROLINE GREW UP IN one of the most well-to-do neighborhoods of Birmingham, Alabama. She grew up in one of those places where the real estate gets so high because of its close proximity to downtown yet somehow stayed away from the decay that crept into most urban areas of America during the latter half of the last century. Her neighborhood looked like everyone who lives there has their lawn manicured by servants. The school system is so good that everyone is expected to become a rocket scientist or a senator if not a doctor or lawyer. I, on the other hand, grew up in the western suburbs of Birmingham, where most lived on a little more modest means and usually cut their own grass. The public education system was sufficient. We aspired to be athletes mostly, not scholars.

My childhood occurred during the time of rapid integration. I was born 804 days after Lyndon Johnson signed the Voting Rights Act of 1965. In 1972 my family moved into a shiny brand new subdivision off of US Highway 78 where they were still clearing trees and framing houses. By the time I reached fifth grade, our neighborhood was nearly an even mix of black and white families with a few South Vietnamese immigrants seeking asylum from the Vietnam War. I grew up in a high school where I was one of two white kids on the basketball team. In the generation before me, my mom had graduated from the same school system in all white classes. Integration was still something of a novelty when we moved to our first home and although my parents were kind and gracious people to everyone they met, they had no African-American friends that I could remember and it might have baffled them, or at least was a curiosity, as to why I played basketball on street courts with all black kids. But there I was, and some of my friends sometimes yelled out, "Hey Oreo!"

My mom was a devout Catholic who married a Baptist sharecropper's son from the rural cotton fields of north Alabama. My dad had had enough of farming and as soon as he graduated from high school moved to the city where he met my mom. Whereas Caroline lived in the upper middle class due to her dad's education and high profile career, my parents never went to college and by the time I was in the 9th grade, I found that I could get no help from them on my homework. But nonetheless they were just as wise as anyone's parents, rich, poor, or somewhere in between. They were married for 53 years before my dad passed away. Only by the grace of God was I born to parents that stayed together and who cared so deeply that I become a well-educated citizen, and who also had the means to provide me every opportunity to become that citizen. Dad went from a hired hand in a warehouse, to buyer for the warehouse, to salesman to many warehouses and gradually clawed his way into the middle class. They knew their roots and by God I was never to buy anything that I couldn't pay for. They never lived above their means and never paid a dime of interest on a credit card.

I never quite understood why the civil rights movement centered on my home state. Caroline never seemed to wonder about these kind of questions nor did any of my friends. But it was one of those curiosities that hung with me for a long time like a sauce simmering on the back burner. After all, there was South Carolina, the first state to leave the Union after the election of Abraham Lincoln; there was Georgia, the last to be readmitted to the Union because they were so slow to ratify the 14th Amendment. So finally, many years later, the movie *Selma* came out and that long standing curiosity bubbled up again. I was there the first week it opened and like most of my basketball days I was the only white dude around.

The Voting Rights Act of 1965 led to far more reaching consequences than just power at the ballot box. I am reminded of the scene in "To Kill a Mockingbird" when Atticus Finch is standing in a courtroom trying to defend an innocent black man in front of an all-white jury during the Jim Crow era. Although the ability to vote is powerful, The Voting Rights Act of 1965 did much more than guarantee suffrage to all Americans equally – it also fulfilled the promises that "the accused shall enjoy the right to...an impartial jury," as granted by the Sixth Amendment to the US Constitution, because being registered to vote also put you on the list to be called for jury duty.

While watching *Selma*, another light bulb went off: I was amazed at how strategic the Southern Christian Leadership Conference was in choosing venues for their civil rights campaign. They were very smart but also incredibly brave and courageous in their analysis of where to go. They chose places where there was controversy and contrast. The belligerence of Dallas County Sheriff Jim Clark towards anyone of color, an African-American woman named Annie Lee Cooper in this specific instance, who dare think they could register to vote within his jurisdiction, did the trick. Martin Luther King, Jr. wasn't trying to change the hearts and minds of the white supremacist; he was trying to tug at the moral consciousness, and thus gain the support of, the white moderate.

The civil rights leaders were also righteous, but not self-righteous. And they were forever hopeful. When Martin Luther King, Jr. said on the steps of the state capital at the end of the second attempt to march to Montgomery, "The arc of the moral universe is long but it bends toward justice," he concisely acknowledged a profound characteristic of the faith he had grown up with in the Sweet Auburn neighborhood of Atlanta that taught him that the general good of the world does prevail. But not without courageous people working in the trenches. It's that timeless teaching that a duality exists between destiny and free will. Our decisions do matter.

WHEN I ENTERED THE park at West Glacier, Montana, on the day before I found fame in The Loop parking lot, so many cars jammed the Sun Road that traffic was in gridlock. I could ride on the shoulder and cruise on past the queue. The Sun Road at the western entrance lies within the Lake McDonald valley, and is surprisingly flat. I could zoom past car after car after car – "Vroom!".....Vroom!".....Vroom!" - in a regular rhythm every 2 seconds. It was so flat that it reminded me of those vacations whereby my mother and father would drag me down to the Florida beaches every single summer and cars would be lined up in both directions on the road that paralleled the edge of the ocean. I never understood why you wanted to sit in a car while on vacation. Wasn't vacation supposed to be, well, a vacation? I had a huge grin on my face and thought, "How cool – a bicycle in the express lane! See you later!"

If you can imagine the straight-away at the bottom of a roller coaster or at the bottom of a ski jump, then you can see how Lake McDonald is nestled within a massive U-shaped notch at the base of the approach to Logan

Pass. In fact, on my approach to the park from the previous night's stay in a campground at Kalispell, Montana, I had only gained 259 feet in elevation over a distance of 56 miles! It was an incredibly easy ride! I kept anticipating, "Where are the big hills?!"

Lake McDonald is a watery remnant of the enormous glacier that filled the entire valley before melting away and receding to the very high alpine areas at the end of the last ice age. At 1 mile wide and over 9 miles long, Lake McDonald is an impressive site and its grandeur appropriately fits to scale among the high, rugged peaks of the Rocky Mountains as though a giant had been using a playset and plopped it down within the seams that run diagonally between the ridges. The Sun Road cuts across the middle of the park by splitting off of US Highway 2, which says "No thank you," dives to the south, hugs the southern border of the park, and crosses the Continental Divide at Marias Pass on its 2,571 mile journey across the northern contiguous US. The Sun Road however, on its way to Logan Pass, runs parallel to the southeastern shoreline of Lake McDonald. It was late in the day when I reached Avalanche Campground above the Lake's upper end the day before. I had been positioning myself for this dash up to Logan Pass and down the other side in one day; due to the curfew, it was important to be right at the base of the steepest part, at the tip top of Lake McDonald, in order to get through the pass and down the other side to the next campground before dark. Whereas the day before when I had approached the park on US Highway 2 comfortably cruising at 12 miles an hour, today I was in the lowest gear slowly grinding my way up the final leg to the Continental Divide at a paltry 2 miles an hour. At that pace, you can walk it as fast as you can peddle it. But the quick, continuous rotation on the tiny front sprocket felt to me like a meditative rhythm. I just couldn't stop without falling over. In sort of a Zen attitude I trained my mind to accept the short, fast peddle strokes that contrasted with the slooooww wheel movement. At first I thought, "Oh my gosh I will be here for days doing this." But then I realized that I made progress little by little and then my mind became attuned, peaceful, and accepting kind of like when a pig settles down into a mud bath. The time passed and before I knew it, the parking lot and the 10 o'clock curfew met in time and space.

The day before, at Avalanche Campground, every campsite had been full – all 87. No surprise after seeing the traffic jam. I had been in a panic though and finally found a ranger.

"What do I do Mam? I can't make it anywhere else before dark – I am on a *bike*!" I exclaimed with despair and as though I rode on something invisible.

She pleasantly smiled and said, "Oh don't worry sweetie, we have a designated spot for non-motorized travelers at *all* of our campgrounds."

My anxiety melted away as she had pointed me in the right direction. The non-motorized campsite was a wide open flat area about the size of a baseball diamond. When I pulled in, the sun was setting, and there were a dozen others there with their tents already set up in no particular pattern. We were surrounded on all sides by families that had pulled into their single, nicely cordoned slots with vehicles towing campers or who had set up big family tents around a grill or fire ring. It was as though we were like a high-density communal park inside a well-planned medium-density subdivision. As I was unpacking the camp stove, a communal camper came over to welcome me like he had known me my whole life, "Hey, whatcha cookin'?"

I dug through my meager 3 day food supply and said, "Oh, let's see here. Probably some rice and tuna?"

"Well my name is Biff!" he said, as he stuck his hand out.

"Biff?"

"Yeah, Biff America! From Breckenridge, Colorado"

Biff's real name was Jeff Bergeron. He was a television personality on a morning show in Breckenridge. He was known as ski country's "David Letterman." Even though I didn't know that at the time, my inclination was to play along;

"Nice to meet you Biff America", as I shook his hand. "Ominous place for you to be. You know - being from ski country and staying in Avalanche Campground?"

I followed it up with a raising of my eyebrows in exaggerated fashion and saying, "Get it?...Get it?...*Avalanche*?" I had a half, insincere smile, then wiped it away quickly as though nothing had happened.

He smiled and then his countenance immediately slacked and you could see the appreciation in his eyes for something I had done that should have been reserved for someone that I knew well. My playfulness would not have set well with most strangers that you had just met. But I had guessed with Biff that it allowed for a quick bond with someone that you didn't have much time to get to know. We were lit up by the fading twilight by the time I had started cooking and so Biff delved right on in and asked, "So, where are you headed from here?"

"Well, I will be out soon after sunrise to get a head-start on the climb over the divide before the 10 o'clock curfew."

"No, I mean on farther."

I pulled out the eleven state maps that I had ripped from a Rand McNally Road Atlas to guide me home. My plan was to do an upside down and inverted

L shaped route that took me through the Great Lakes Region and then turn south at the Straights of Mackinac.

"Well, won't you be going through Traverse City, Michigan?"

"I don't know. Right now I am just sticking to US Highway 2."

"Yeah, I am pretty sure you will be going through Traverse City. Will you deliver a note to my friend there?"

"Sure...I guess," I replied hesitantly.

Biff scribbled on an index card, including a phone number, and handed it to me. It said, "Hanz: you stud! Hope all is well. Please let this guy take a shower 'he need it' Remind him to wash his feets. Love Biff"

I FINALLY MADE IT through Logan Pass with just enough daylight left to get to the Rising Sun Campground but cooked supper in the dark. Less than two weeks earlier I had gone through Stevens Pass in the Cascade Mountains on the first day; luckily I was able to go from the coast, up the west side, through the pass, and down the other side in one day, and had supper cooked before dark. Such a long first day wasn't really my plan. Though the first day of summer had passed already, it was shocking to see snow still covering much of the road and peaks around Stevens Pass. Signs read, "Remote area. Hitchhiking permitted." It was eerily quiet, no one was around, visibility was literally foggy, the sky was completely covered in clouds, and my skin had goose bumps from the both the chill in the air and the utter desolation. With no direct sunlight nothing had any color to it and it looked as though I was watching a black and white film. I saw ski lift chairs hanging motionless as though everyone had suddenly abandoned the place. I expected Freddie Kruger to pop out at any moment.

But the climb to Logan Pass was quite different. As the park's website puts it, "The average gradient for this section of the ride is roughly 5.7%. To put those numbers in perspective, L'Alpe d'Huez, one of the most famous and notoriously difficult climbs in the Tour de France, climbs roughly 3770 feet (and) has an average gradient of 7.6%. It's likely the Going-to-the-Sun Road climb would rank among the top 20 toughest climbs in the Tour de France, and would likely be a category 1 climb." It made the climb to Stevens Pass seem like a small nuisance of a hill, and Stevens Pass made the population density of Logan Pass, with all its tourists, seem like a metropolis.

It took two and one-half hours to pedal eight miles to the refuge at The Loop. I had teamed up with two other bikers at Avalanche Campground and we locked our bikes together in the parking lot and took a hike. We got back on our bikes at 4pm and rode another 8 miles to Logan Pass. The Rocky

Mountains are generally shaped like a very unequal, highly skewed, and tilted wedge. While Lake McDonald is snuggled in at 3200 feet above sea level on the west side of the divide, Lake Mary is nestled in its analogous U-shaped valley on the east side 1600 feet higher. And whereas it is a 16 mile climb from the head of Lake McDonald to Logan Pass it is half that distance from Logan Pass to the head of Lake Mary. The uplift that created the ridge of the Continental Divide is made from rock that stair steps its way up beginning in Spokane, Washington. It is 200 miles as the crow flies from Spokane to Logan Pass and here is how the elevations read, in feet above sea level, along US Highway 2 from west to east:

Spokane, WA:	1,843
Priest River, ID:	2,139
Kalispell, MT:	2,956
West Glacier, MT:	3,215
Logan Pass:	6,647

The mountains then abruptly end 20 miles east of the Continental Divide. It took 4 days to wind my way up the western slopes after leaving Spokane. We coasted down to Rising Sun Campground, and within a rock's throw of the Great Plains, in a half hour.

SIXTEEN YEARS LATER, IN 2007, the park service would start free shuttle service to help relieve some of the congestion. In the meantime, the world continues to consume roughly 80 million barrels of oil a day, every day, 365 days a year.[3] You can go to the US Energy Information Administration's website where they publish weekly reports that say things like, "US crude oil refinery inputs averaged 16.6 million barrels per **day** during the week ending August 5, 2016...." Unless some of the fuel made from the refinery process is put in storage, which is sometimes the case, 16.6 million barrels is how much we actually used that week. Another statement in the report says, "US crude oil imports averaged 8.4 million barrels per day last week..." If you take 16.6 minus 8.4, then you get the amount of oil that we consumed that was produced domestically. In this case the answer would be 8.2 million barrels a day. The proportion of oil consumed in the US and that was produced domestically for the week of August 5, 2016 would be roughly half.

The debate over whether or not to drill in the Alaska's Arctic National Wildlife Refuge pits one side arguing that it is needed to increase domestic supply and drive down prices versus the other side arguing to protect wildlife migration corridors. Both sides probably have it wrong. What is most likely contributing the overwhelming majority of loss of wildlife populations and creating species' extinctions is urbanization, suburbanization, and the conversion of natural habitat into farmland...not a linear, narrow, elevated pipeline corridor running across an eight million acre wilderness.[4] On the other side of the debate, the amount of extractable reserves in the ground in the Alaskan wilderness would probably drop the price of gasoline at the pumps by about...wait for it...five cents a gallon! It's because there is nothing patriotic about the location from which the oil is extracted. It still has to compete within world markets.[5] I think that the real policy debate should include questions like, "How are we going to diversify our transportation network?", "How are we going to ease the inevitable transition of jobs from one energy sector to another?", "How are we going to allocate resources to mitigate the future effects of a warming climate in order to protect the public welfare?".... "And how are we going to do all this while keeping our nation solvent?"

Going-to-the-Sun Road in the Lake McDonald Valley

Lake McDonald

College Park, Georgia

College Park Transit and Pedestrian Ways

- Bike/Ped Paths
- Heavy Rail Line
- Blue Line (Bus Routes)
- Green Line
- Orange Line
- Purple Line
- Red Line
- Yellow Line
- Monorail

Willingham
East Main
Vesta
Mercer
Harrison N.
Rugby
Virginia
Lee
Adams
Myrtle
Madison
Harrison S.
John Calvin
Library/City Hall
Harvard/Depot
Aerotropolis
Center
Herschel North
Global Gateway N.
GICC South
Best Rd / Phoenix Trail
HJAIA
DQ
lobal Gateway S.
hel South
Greenspring
Sullivan
O.N. Bus. District
Godby
N Pkwy
Limetree
Scofield
Norman
Southampton West
Jones Circle
Southampton East
W Fayetteville Rd
Phoenix West
Phoenix East
Riverdale Rd

0   0.25   0.5   1 Miles

N

Ninety-eight percent of U.S. commuters favor public transportation for others.
– *The Onion*

STANDING AT THE BUS stop in January in short sleeves probably did kind of look out of place. But I had spent three winters in northern Minnesota near the Canadian border, and winter in metro Atlanta just felt to me like a nice, cool transition out of summer. Sometimes when I get on the bus, I make my way to the rear so that I can open a window to get relief from the roaring heater. If the outside temperature on a June day were as hot as the temperature inside a MARTA bus in January, I am pretty sure the A/C would have been roaring instead.

The *mountains* of Georgia are a different story however. They have four seasons no doubt. I had also just spent a weekend in the backcountry of a remote wilderness area around a place called Tate City camping in a foot and a half of snow. The highest ridgelines have the same ecosystem as northeastern Minnesota, whose forest canopy is dominated by spruce and fir trees, understory by Red Osier Dogwood, and is carpeted with Canada Mayflower in the summer.

The bus driver pulled up and opened the door and looked down at me from his perch up on the driver's seat and matter-of-factly stated, "Mista Duke, you got ice water runnin' through yo veins."

The next week I was standing at the same stop and I had forgotten my transit card. I stepped on and said, "Sir I forgot my card."

With a straight face, the same bus driver who had called me by name just a few days earlier very formally pointed at the fare box and turned his head away and his chin up so indignantly that it was as if he didn't know me. I promptly opened my wallet and dug for some change in my pocket and dropped the dollar bill and coins into the appropriate slots. The machine gave an approving "ding!" The bus driver nodded and I proceeded down the aisle. There were no open seats and everyone was staring at me. That is the way it goes when you are the only white guy on the bus and you are wearing a tie. As the bus made its way towards my office the seats slowly began to clear out and I was able to sit down the last few miles. The bus was nearly empty when I pulled the cord to ring the next-to-last stop on the route. As I neared the bus's front door, the driver put out his arm and stopped me. He leaned over in his seat, pulled out his wallet from his back pocket, and handed me a dollar and fifty cents.

"Don't forget your card tomorrow!" he said quickly and sternly.

Bus systems are the backbone of most cities' public transportation network around the world. Bus lines get replaced with rail only when the buses start to run at full capacity. Bus comes first then rail. Not the other way around. For example, the *Baltimore Sun* accused their own town of not being a transit city. When I visited that fair city at my step-daughter's graduation from Johns

Hopkins University I had no problem and had figured out the whole network of bus routes by the second day. For four dollars and twenty-five cents I hopped on and off all day long and never waited longer than 7 minutes. Oh what the heck - I just threw in a five dollar bill; keep the change. In San Francisco you ride the Muni buses to get around efficiently, not the BARTA train system. In my own home town, the complaint is that MARTA doesn't go anywhere, which isn't true; the buses actually do go everywhere and they are part of MARTA just like the train. In fact some bus lines run *faster* than the train.

The bus I used to get to work left the East Point train station, went down Main Street, and then turned east towards Hapeville on Willingham Drive, at which I caught it, 10 blocks from my house in College Park. When it crossed the Clayton County line, whether you had paid for a monthly card or not, everyone had to pay a 75 cent surcharge. The City of Forest Park, in the northern part of Clayton County, had always had public transit. When the Atlanta metro counties voted to join MARTA in 1972 Clayton County as a whole said, "No thanks." But Forest Park said, "Wait a minute... we have always had it. Just because the county says no doesn't mean that we mean no." MARTA's viewpoint was, "Sorry, you aren't contributing anything to a 6 billion dollar infrastructure project to upgrade to train lines and robust bus service." An agreement was reached whereby one bus line from the East Point train station would cross the Fulton-Clayton line but not for free. Anyone getting off in Clayton had to drop seventy-five cents into the fare box and anyone using a MARTA transit card to get on the bus from inside Clayton had to drop an extra seventy-five cents into the fare box. It was why we always had to leave the bus by the front door when in Clayton County. Normally passengers entered at the front door by the fare box while exiting passengers left through the back door, and the bus driver had control of which doors could be opened. Nonetheless, the "MARTA-north Clayton" fare structure arrangement was probably a fair deal for the citizens and businesses of Forest Park. While the core metro counties (Fulton and DeKalb) who *did* join the system were throwing in hundreds of millions of dollars a year into the system generated from a dedicated 1% sales tax, Forest Park could continue to receive service through this "cash only" surcharge system. New or infrequent riders didn't understand this. We regulars sometimes had to explain it to them:

Occasionally, a regular such as *me* got caught without the change to pay the surcharge. You didn't mind losing a quarter if you had to put a dollar bill in, but you certainly didn't want to put a five dollar bill in. I got to know a lady because we saw each other every morning and she got off the bus a few stops before me inside the Clayton County line. One day, having neither any change nor any dollar bills, I asked if she had seventy-five cents that I could borrow to get off the bus.

She said, "Of course!"

The next day I re-paid her. A few weeks later she asked me to borrow seventy-five cents.

I said, "Sure!"

She would pay me back and this went on for a while. Sometimes the paybacks would be delayed but we kept an informal estimated tally in our heads. On one occasion, a "first timer" was on the bus and he didn't have the required seventy-five cents. He innocently tried to exit out of the back door, and when it wouldn't open he yelled,

"Back door!"

The bus driver yelled back, "Front door, please!"

He walked to the front, stared at the unopened front door, and turned around to the driver who was pointing at the fare box. This was a frustrating experience for those of us who may have been running late to work. My lady friend glanced over at me from across the bus and pointed towards the fare box. Somehow we both knew that I was the one behind the eight ball. She was indicating that she wanted me to pay-forward the seventy-five cents that I owed her by giving it to the "newcomer." As the bus driver was trying to explain, I walked up and dropped three quarters in the fare box, looked at the driver, and nodded my head. The bus driver nodded in return and opened the door.

I MOVED BACK TO College Park from Minnesota in January 2010. I had owned a home in the historic district since 1998 and while I was away in Ely, Minnesota for those 3 years, flight attendants and pilots had rented rooms in the house. They were such great tenants that I usually became good friends with them and would actually stay in the house in whatever room was empty or if necessary, on the couch, on those infrequent occasions that I visited. If you have ever taken the train out of Hartsfield-Jackson Atlanta International Airport, College Park is the first stop on the line to downtown Atlanta. In Ely I was living next to a 2-million acre wilderness but paradoxically felt almost claustrophobic. When I made the decision to return to my home, I declared that I would never leave it again. I started working part-time for Porter Alexander at Urban Solutions, a College Park city planning firm, doing a variety of tasks including environmental permitting, hydrology studies, conceptual designs, floodplain analysis, and geographical data management.

Porter and I had met when I was serving on the College Park Board of Zoning Appeals. Porter was contracted by the city to, among other duties, be the liaison between the applicant requesting a zoning variance and the board. He would also make a recommendation as to whether it would be prudent to approve the applicant's request or deny it. We didn't have to take his recommendation. In fact, on some occasions, I would disagree with his recommendation and sometimes would be successful in leading the charge to go against it. We never took things personal in those meetings and could be seen many times having a beer together afterwards at a local pub.

The board was made up of five members, one appointed from each councilman and one appointed by the mayor. I started on the board as the representative from Ward 3. But after a political shake-up in my ward, the newly incumbent councilman kicked me off. I never missed a beat in the 3 years I served because the mayor's appointee had to leave his post at the same time and I was immediately put back on the board as his appointment the very next meeting.

My last meeting before leaving for Minnesota, I had opposed Porter's recommendation. He said the variance request should be denied for a reduction in parking space requirements for a new restaurant on Virginia Avenue. It was to be located about two blocks from the campus of Woodward Academy, the second largest private K-12 school in the country. The restaurant was connected by sidewalks to the school and to a large chunk of residential housing in Ward 3. Virginia Avenue had frequent and all night bus service down Virginia Avenue that was the sweeper between two train stations. Furthermore, it was already going to have a quarter-acre parking lot even with the variance and would have access to public parking along the side streets. I felt the applicant had a legitimate hardship in wanting to make his restaurant larger and the parking lot smaller. It was being built up to the sidewalk and the parking was being moved to the side and back. I thought it was a good looking plan. The councilman from Ward 3 was not about to let me have my way and made it clear at public comment. There was much debate by everyone on the board and I had no idea how the vote might go. After a very long discussion, I finally made the motion to allow the variance. Someone else took the bold move to second my motion so that it could go for a full vote. The chairperson of the board said,

"We have a motion and a second. Any more discussion?"

Silence

"All in favor?"

There was a chorus of "Aye's."

"All opposed?"

There was also a chorus of "Nay's."

Then the chairperson declared, "The ayes have it. For the record, let it be known that Ward 2 and Ward 4 opposed."

The person in Ward 3, who had been appointed to sit in the seat that I had been kicked off of, had seconded my motion and the chairperson broke the tie.

If you ever go to one of those zoning board meetings still today, there is honest debate about the issues. If those appointed boards are autonomous, whereby the decisions stand on their own and without oversight from the governing body, they are strong democratic institutions. There is no grand standing, and by and large, the ethics are solid, community values are met, and the right thing is almost always done. There is a chance for vibrant participatory democracy at the local level where people have a chance to feel empowered. It sustains our whole country. Our communities, of which there are thousands, act in much the same way as a capillary does in our bodies; they are the "functional unit of society" carrying out a vital task. It's where things get done at the microscopic level and where governments are forced to set priorities in order to balance the budget. They are constantly under great pressure to accomplish this and it can create some lively discussions.

Politics at the national level, on the other hand, is almost lethargic by comparison. How many times in a primary debate are issues discussed if ever? There are hyperbolic, philosophical discussions about what policy should look like but the real nuts and bolts of it seem to rarely get hammered out. The discussions look like people falling over themselves to cater to the extreme views at either end of the base support. And there is absolutely no intention of the federal government to ever balance the budget. It's as though the federal government has become the "backstop" for debt accumulation. In other words, it seems the federal government is where all the debt in the nation from our cumulative choices in the economy eventually lands. Everyone else needs to balance their budget from individuals to local governments to state governments, and if you can't or you need financing, we, the feds, or maybe a private institution backed by the feds, will hold the note for you. And that is not all bad. The federal government is like the rich uncle funding your college education. It allows for freedom of ideas which leads to economic expansion. It also allows for a safety net when things happen that are beyond our control. But eventually there has to be accountability. The only reason we haven't reached that point yet is because the world thinks this is still the coolest place on the planet and they feel safe to park any extra cash they might have right here because it would be safe. If it weren't safe, U.S. Treasury Bonds wouldn't constantly hover around 2%. Those low rates are only sustainable by our trust and goodwill. The scary thing is that our economy might collapse *not* if people around the world wanted to cash in on the bonds we are holding. It would happen a step *earlier*. You have to understand that the federal government would not even be able to make payroll if people, corporations, and governments from here and abroad simply stopped investing in treasury bonds. Because current federal budgets are in constant deficit spending, they are dependent on *current* cash flow into bonds today! It is a mind boggling proposition.

The National Commission of Fiscal Responsibility and Reform, also known as The Simpson-Bowles Plan, was released about the time I moved back to College Park and offered common sense solutions. But nothing has been done. Status quo has been maintained and will be maintained into the foreseeable future. The two-party system just has it too good. The duopoly has evolved to the point of equilibrium where power is almost evenly divided between the two parties. There is no incentive whatsoever to change that. Would you if you were the beneficiary of that wealth of power? There are media outlets that thrive on the polarization and are making way too much money to rock the boat and provide alternative viewpoints to the Democratic-Republican narrative either. Current political campaigns discuss how you would get this tax advantage if you vote for this candidate or that tax advantage if you vote for the other candidate. In other words, the current tax code is really smoke and mirrors. There is no honesty and transparency in the tax code that we can all understand. Under the recommendations by the Commission, the tax code would be rid of 1 trillion dollars in tax expenditures and there would be a fighting chance to create a real budget that eventually leads to solvency. Any tax expenditure that we would like to keep would have to be voted on by Congress as part of the yearly budgetary process and would remain outside the realm of an unelected bureaucracy. You might pay more or you might pay less than what you paid under the current system. But it's honest. And the point is...it forces you to participate in democracy again like you do at the local level.[6]

The author at West Glacier, Montana

Hudson Bay Divide

A Pass With No Name

IMMEDIATELY AFTER SLICING BETWEEN the peaks at Logan Pass, you enter into a wedge of land inside the U.S. that is about half the size of Rhode Island, where the streams generally flow north. It's one of the three places in the U.S. where this happens and I would hit all of them during my ride across the continent. This wedge of land is formed from two ridges. One ridge, the (Western) Continental Divide[7] runs north and south through the Rocky Mountains and is the one that I had transected the day before at Logan Pass. The other ridge runs roughly east and west between the Rockies and the Great Lakes, mostly in Canada but at times dipping across the border; its official name is The Laurentian Divide but informally goes by The Hudson Bay Divide. It so nearly follows the US-Canadian border that it seems the logical thing to do might have been to follow this natural ridge when establishing the political border between the two countries than to argue over an arbitrarily designated latitude line.

Thus, as soon as you leave out of Glacier National Park you slowly begin to climb again. I was confused and started to question myself. Various thoughts and emotions raced through my head. Ethan and Angela were my companions from California whom I had ridden with over Logan Pass the day before. We had arrived at Rising Sun Campground so late the night before we didn't get through cleaning up supper dishes until almost 11 o'clock. One reason was that in fact there was *not* a biker/hiker spot reserved in the completely full campground and the ranger had to open up an area for us that had been closed off. We had bonded through the ordeal of a day that could not have possibly encompassed any more in 24 hours. Today we stopped in the town of St Mary to get a few supplies, do a bit of laundry, and now toiled up yet another hill. No one could go very fast so we stayed close. No wind blew, no birds sang, no cars passed, and it was so quiet that I could hear my companions breathing. I was angry, weary, hungry, and elated all at the same time. Angry that I was on a hill, weary from days of uphill climbing, hungry from a chronic calorie deficit, and elated to finally be with riding companions.

I finally yelled out in exasperation that seemed like it should echo across the barren landscape but in fact became absorbed and muffled by the still, empty air, "I thought we already left the mountains and were heading into the flat wide open plains?!"

"We might be approaching the Hudson Bay Divide," Ethan offered.

"I thought we exited the park below the divide?" I hopefully retorted.

Angela then stopped riding and we all pulled to the side of the road together. She got her map out and after figuring out where we were exactly said somberly, "Yeah it's another divide."

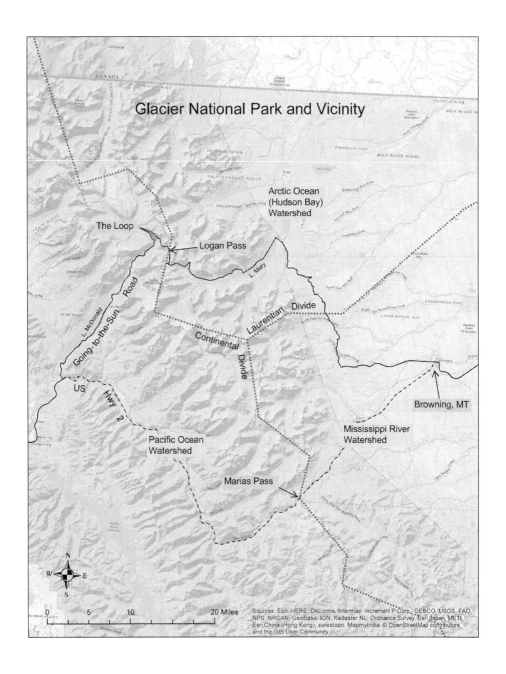

Glacier National Park and Vicinity

The area seemed so stale because we were within the rain shadow of the Rocky Mountains. As warm moisture is drawn off of the surface of the Pacific Ocean and forms into clouds, they generally blow east. When the moisture laden clouds hit the wall of the Rockies, they have nowhere to go but up. Cold air cannot hold water very well; as the clouds rise, the air cools and all the moisture falls out. Therefore, the west side of Logan Pass almost looks like a cool, refreshing rain forest and on the east side the vegetation appears stunted. Whereas big spruce and fir trees dominate the canopy in a mature alpine forest towering overhead at Logan Pass, here runt trees looked like stick figures with stubby arms almost at eye-level height. Whereas the groundcover at Logan Pass was lush and dense, here there were bare, brown patches of eroded soil with dry channels carved out by the infrequent bursts of rain.

To make it more confusing, I could see no mountains ahead of me. We were just facing a dull paved incline in front of us. The air was at a complete standstill and I felt, although dry, uncomfortably stuffy. I thought, "Are we *really* climbing just one big isolated hill out in the middle of nowhere?!" This happened to be the exact spot where the Laurentian Divide made a quick dive across the Canadian border and into the United States and where it continued on to T into the Continental Divide at a summit inside the park called Triple Divide Peak. The T forms three wedges of a pie. The western wedge drains to the Pacific Ocean, the eastern wedge drains to the Mississippi River, and the smaller northern wedge drains to the Arctic Ocean. We had fallen inside the northern wedge after crossing Logan Pass the day before. We had dropped into a little nook that happened to empty towards the top of the globe and were now climbing our way up and over in order to get back into the Mississippi drainage basin. Now I knew why the major transportation corridor had been built through Marias Pass – why go over two passes when you can accomplish the same thing with one? When I turned out of the park on Highway 89 towards Browning, Montana, I had thought we had smooth sailing on flat, wide open roads for the next 900 miles. Now we found ourselves slowly grinding uphill at two miles an hour...again. We were climbing back up to the "U.S." side of the Laurentian Divide and after five miles we finally reached the pass that didn't even have a name! So we all got off of our bicycles and stood in the middle of the desolate road bellowing the poetry from a 70's band named *America* that could best describe the contrasting landscape over the past two days. One day we were in a lush forest and the next we were in a desert.

Angela then suggested that we stay down a dirt road that dives back into the park from its eastern edge to a place called Cut Bank Campground. Not surprisingly, that campground was full too. Except in this remote part of the park there was no ranger to appeal to. I was tired of muscling the heavy bicycle around on the 5-mile long entrance road that sometimes made the tires sink in. It took nearly an hour to get to the campground once we left the pavement. I wanted to just relax and have one of the beers we had bought from the grocery store in St Mary.

"Now what do we do?" I asked. "Go back to the main road?"

As Ethan was contemplating the map, he said, "Well it looks like..."

He was interrupted by Angela, "Hey guys there is a fellow over there waiving at us."

A man with black hair and brown skin had his arms in the air and was staring us down. "You guys looking for a place to pull in!?" he yelled across the rode with his hands cupped around his mouth.

He was the father of a Native American family from the Blackfeet Reservation and not only was he offering his spot but he also wanted us to have the leftovers from their day's picnic. They were about to go home and we ate so much of their food while we listened to his stories that we didn't even bother to cook supper that night.

The next day we stopped again at a grocery store in Browning, a quiet town on the edge of the prairies in the middle of the Blackfeet Reservation. I saw subtle signs of utter abject poverty – rusted out cars, run down mobile homes - some burned out. Some of the same tribe of people who had fed us the day before was now asking us for money and/or food while we packed our groceries. I felt embarrassed that I had taken food from some of these same people the night before and now they were asking me for help. How could I not buy food for those who asked? We went back in the store and nearly spent as much on others as we did on our own supplies. We ate lunch near the Museum of the Plains Indian and then afterwards Angela and Ethan began the journey back to California by turning towards Marias Pass. As I pedaled away, I turned to catch one last glimpse of them, waved goodbye, and have never seen them since.

The rain shadow of the Cascades has a similar look and feel as the dry climate east of the Rockies

The Great Plains

"Ain't this place a geographical oddity – two weeks from everywhere!"
– Ulysses Everett McGill, *O Brother, Where Art Though?*

THE LAND TO THE east of Glacier National Park is called the "high" plains for good reason. At Browning, Montana, headquarters of the Blackfeet Indian Reservation and where I reconnected with US Highway 2, the elevation is 4,377 feet. Browning is higher than many peaks along the Appalachian Trail. But in Browning, it is as flat as a table top. It's as though the flat ground has been lifted up along the base of a wall known as the eastern side of the Rockies. There was a blue sky on the morning I left the park on US Highway 89 leading to Browning with my back to the mountains. It occurred to me to take a moment and see what was behind me. So I pulled over, got off the bicycle, and slowly turned around. I stood looking due west and 11 miles as the crow flies from the border of the park with my mouth slightly gaping open. The stark contrast between the bluish 10,000 foot peaks of the Rocky Mountains that were illuminated by the rising sun behind me and the dry, brown, sandy, wide-open, nearly treeless landscape in front of me was extraordinarily impressive. The 2-lane highway was just a meaningless, almost un-noticeable, thin linear piece of slithering black asphalt that ran off and disappeared into the distance in the middle of a wide frame that extended beyond the limits of your peripheral vision. You had to sweep your head from side to side as if visualizing a panorama to take it all in. "Bye-bye mountains. I will miss you."

Five days and 422 miles later, I pulled into Culbertson, Montana. My friend from college, JJ, worked on a beef farm in the vicinity as a seasonal hand. Culbertson is located in Roosevelt County, population 10,425. It is dry ranch country and in this area of the plains, though vistas still seem to extend to the horizon, there is some rolling undulation that begins to provide some variety to the flat and wide open landscape. Population density is 4.4 people per square mile. In 1993, Dayton Duncan wrote a book called *Miles From Nowhere* that debunks the myth that the American frontier had been declared over in 1890. He traveled to several counties west of the Mississippi River and interviewed people who still today live in places that have less than 2 people per square mile, the definition of a frontier that had been arbitrarily set by the US Census Bureau. Roosevelt County has over twice the density of these places he visited and *it* was pretty desolate. The only reason that Roosevelt County didn't fall into the frontier category was because of the lifeblood of the railroad, US Highway 2, and the Missouri River. There were 23 counties in Montana that were classified as frontier when I rode through the state in 1991. Most of them are east of the Rockies and I hit four of them along the Hi-Line, the common name for this major transportation corridor running just south of the Canadian border from Spokane to Minnesota. Their total population has dropped another 7% today. Agriculture - wheat, barley, and cattle - comprises almost the entire economy and little did I know that I would soon experience it firsthand and become a part of it.

Even though it is several hundred miles from Glacier National Park to Culbertson, they still lie within the rain shadow and usually receive only about 12 inches of rain a year. I had slowly dropped 2400 feet in elevation since leaving Browning but had never noticed it. It was such a flat and open landscape that I saw the white sides of buildings in most towns of Montana three miles before I arrived. Once in town, I could fill my water bottles at the local park and get some shade because it was the only place where trees had been planted. The wind had been in my face and at times I had been counting pedal strokes to break up the monotony.

I found a pay phone, deposited one single dime, and dialed JJ's number. Someone said that he would have to call back. I gave them the number on the pay phone and waited. About 10 minutes later the phone rang.

"JJ?" I asked unconfidently.

"Yeah, it's me. Where are you?"

"In town...Culbertson. You can't miss me. How about meeting me at The Coach Lounge?"

"Be there in about an hour," he replied.

"OK. I will be waiting."

The population of Culbertson is 779. Like most towns across the great plains of Montana north of the Missouri River, US Highway 2 is "Main Street" and usually runs less than a mile long. In Culbertson, US 2 is called 6th Street though. Back in Chester, it was called Washington Avenue. In Havre, Chinook, Malta, and Glasgow it was 1st Street. In Harlem it was Central Avenue. And at Wolf Point, the county seat of Roosevelt County, and which has the largest community of Native Americans on the Fort Peck Indian Reservation, it's just US Highway 2. The total population of those 8 towns, which string out like widely spaced beads on a string, is about half of the number of people at a college football game on a typical fall Saturday.[8] It is not hard to be found.

All of these towns were originally built as farming settlements along the Great Northern Railway and US Highway 2 came later as a parallel thoroughfare. It is thought that this railway inspired the fictional Taggart Transcontinental Railroad by the author Ayn Rand.[9] Against the backdrop of the wide open plains of Montana and the endless sky, the train cars look like block toys. One day a freight train tapped its horn at me in a gesture of "hello." This brief human to human connection, though in the distance and from someone I couldn't even see, inspired more emotional bond inside me on this lonely stretch of highway than any of the characters ever could in *Atlas*

Shrugged. There are silos to store grain in every town along the railroad line where freight cars empty them and haul the cash crops away to coastal ports. Today, Amtrak shares the line transporting people between the Midwest and Seattle, with stops on each side of Glacier National Park. Its route is aptly called the Empire Builder; Rand's protagonist, Dagny Taggart, would have liked that.

RAIL TRAVEL, INCLUDING BOTH passenger and freight trains, accounts for 1% of all greenhouse gas emissions in the US. On the other hand, vehicles, anything from cars to delivery trucks but not including 18-wheeler freight trucks, is #3 out of 13 in US greenhouse gas inventories and create eight times more than all the jet airplanes taking off every day.[10] Let's face it, everybody loves cheap gas. But in early 2015, Christophe McGlade and Paul Ekins, in the journal *Nature*, implied that not only will we *not* run out of gas, at least not in our lifetime, but that we should probably just leave at least a third of the world's oil supply just lying there in the ground. Just let it sit![11]

Ecological principle number 1 is that the energy I use to propel my bicycle and the energy used to run a gasoline engine both began as solar radiation. It gets converted from one form to another and along the way all of it is eventually lost as heat, which is released back into outer space. The difference between me and the car is that I am using "real time" energy. I ate some beans and rice that were grown within the past year and converted the stored energy to pedal my bicycle. As I pedaled, everything was used up and converted into heat, which went into the air and escaped our planet into outer space through the atmosphere. If you heat a house with a wood burning stove, you are also using real time energy. The tree had been storing away energy from when the sun shone on it during the past 20 or 30 years before it got cut down. You burn the stored energy in your stove during the cold winter, and at the same time another tree somewhere is taking in CO2 and storing away more energy. If all this is managed correctly, and we don't denude the trees too much so that they can't replace themselves, it works out pretty good. However, burning oil releases energy that had been stored by what were plants and that were buried, compressed, and that have been sitting dormant within the crust of the earth for millions of years.

Ecological principle number 2 is that no molecules, such as carbon, oxygen, or water, can ever go off into outer space. (Nor can any enter.) Theoretically, not one single atom. One thing that allows life to exist on the planet is the fact that the atmosphere is like a dome that holds everything in and keeps out harmful UV radiation. All of these different molecules can hit the dome's underside but will bounce back towards the earth. They can get redistributed and moved around the planet but they can never leave. We can actually measure how much there are of all these molecules and track where they currently reside. For carbon, about 1000 billion tons has dissolved into the surface waters of the oceans, there are about 1,500 billion tons in the microbes and decaying plant matter within the soil, the atmosphere holds about 800 billion tons, and there are about 600 billion tons in plants. All of these reservoirs of carbon are fluid and dynamic. Carbon readily moves around these four places on a daily basis.

Imagine all of the credit card machines at stores and banks that are moving cash around every day in order to operate our economy. But what if someone added extra money into the economic system every day? Inflation would eventually get out of control. When we are not burning carbon in real time, we are adding to these four main carbon "players." And so we have figured out that you can budget carbon just like you can budget your checkbook. The average annual global temperature before the industrial revolution was less than 57 degrees F. In 2015, the hottest year on record at the time, the average annual global temperature was 59 degrees F. We have about 1000 billion tons of carbon left we can burn from fossil fuels to keep the average annual global temperature below 61 degrees F. By comparison, Mars' atmosphere is so flimsy, $1/100^{th}$ as thick as earth's, it can hold in only enough heat to keep the surface at an average temperature of *negative* 57 degrees F. Venus, on the other hand, has a thick atmosphere made of mostly CO2 and has a near constant temperature of 878 degrees F. Our moon has no atmosphere, thus has a hard time even regulating heat, and fluctuates from a scorching 257 degrees during the day to an almost unbelievable -258 degrees at night.[12]

For earth, what does a one-degree change mean? During the last ice age that created the glaciers that carved out the Lake McDonald Valley, the average annual global temperature was 48 degrees F, about 9 degrees colder than today. Minnesota was covered in a sheet of ice one mile thick. Some of the ice still exists – it just has retreated northward and now sits in northern Canada. There were still four seasons (outside the tropics) just like today. However, so much precipitation fell over centuries of time and never got returned to the oceans because it remained frozen that ocean levels dropped so much so that the Bering Sea became a wide plain covered in snow in the winter and covered in grass in the summer; think of a cold Serengeti ecosystem between Alaska and Russia where today there is a 53-mile wide, 130-foot deep gap covered by salt water. To keep the planet cool, not only will we have to leave a third of the world's oil reserves in the ground, we also have to keep half of the natural gas reserves buried, and 80% of the coal reserves intact.

I WENT TO THE RANCH with JJ that night. I had no idea where we were. We drove somewhere towards the Missouri River, which I never saw, and I don't remember seeing another house or even another car the whole way. Every once in a while we would slow down to drive across cattle guards that would make the tires rumble. Cattle guards were created to allow a break in the fence where public roads transected the fence line and no gate exists. They look like stormwater drains with parallel slats that sit level with the grade of the road; the idea is that cattle won't walk across them. I remember straining to see out the windshield as the headlights illuminated the dust in the air ahead of us. The small piece of road inside the beam of the headlights was framed in pitch black darkness. When we finally arrived, JJ said, "Oh yeah, we are moving cattle to fall pastureland tomorrow."

"In July?"

"Yeah, winter here starts sometime in October. Want to help or do you want to hang here?"

"I'm with you."

"We will put you on a horse then to help push the herd along."

"Cool!"

"Breakfast is at sunrise."

They put me on a chestnut Appaloosa-Thoroughbred mixed gelding named Clyde. We moved 250 cows and their calves for 12 miles. About half the route took us across wide open rangeland and the other half of the route literally went down the middle of a dirt county road bordered on both sides by fencing. Clyde mostly walked the whole way but every once in a while on the open rangeland a calf would mindlessly stray off to the side and I had to nudge Clyde into a light trot to head the calf off from wandering God-knows-where and redirect it's course back towards the herd. I could see the dumbfounded calf turn its eyes and also its head slightly to the side as if to say "Where did you come from?" and then it would bolt back into the herd usually with its back feet kicked up into the air as it pushed off.

The ranch spanned across 20,000 acres that included the bottomland floodplain of the Missouri River, where big Cottonwood trees grow. It also included the rolling plains of the high range and sometimes in between the bottomlands and high range you can find the badlands that are a unique feature to this part of the continent. The badlands consist of patches of exposed rock, and if you ever wondered what it would be like to stand on the moon, this is as close as it might feel. The ranch was totally self-contained. JJ told me that when it was time for him to leave, they would load up the wheat truck with grain and drive it into Culbertson to be sold. This marketing task would generate about 2500 dollars' worth of cash to pay JJ at summer's end.

The farm grew wheat, barley, and oats as commodity crops to be sold. The farm also had its own feedlot, which was key in making it totally self-sufficient. Most operations that raise beef calves ship them off when they are weaned at 3-4 months old to Iowa or Kansas or somewhere else in the Midwest where either rainfall or an underground aquifer provides more plentiful water as compared to Montana and where they can grow enormous quantities of corn. The weaned calves eat corn for about a year and then are shipped a second time to the packing house. The calves raised on JJ's ranch however were shipped only once. The ranch grew corn and safflower but had the advantage of being able to draw irrigation water from the Missouri River. Once harvested, these crops were placed in earthen fermentation pits and made into cattle feed called *silage* - probably a similar process to making sauerkraut from cabbage - and thereby preserving it for the coming winter. Instead of shipping calves to a feedlot in the Midwest, the silage was fed to the calves once they were weaned. The commodity grains, also referred to as "dry crops" and "cash crops", could then utilize the highland because they would normally thrive in the relatively dry climate without irrigation. There was a small plot of irrigated land around the house that grew vegetables to be canned for the winter. Probably about 50% of the ranch's total food demand was met by everything produced on site. The rest was bought in town with some of the beef and dry crop revenues.

The cows could satisfactorily utilize the grasses growing on the open range during the frost free months of the year for all of their caloric needs. East of the Mississippi River one cow can maintain itself and produce milk for a growing calf on one or two acres of grassland. In Montana, due to the parched conditions, it takes about 60 acres per cow. Besides growing grains and silage, some of the ranch was also used to produce hay for the cows during the winter months. By the time winter came a cow's caloric requirement was reduced because the calf had been weaned. But those caloric requirements were replaced with the energy needed to survive a cold Montana winter. During the summer, when grass was abundant, she needed to not only produce milk, which itself is four times more caloric demanding than pregnancy, but also put away fat stores. When we finally reached our destination and had turned those cows out on their new green field, they immediately put their heads down and slowly walked as they devoured the blades of green grass. Not only did the green grass provide calories, it was succulent enough to provide a bit of water stored in the grass blades. They say that a cow on the western rangeland has to walk 1 mile an hour all day long to stay alive. Before October, the calves would be rounded up and sent to the feedlot, bulls would be released, and a new crop of calves would hopefully be born the following spring.

IN CULBERTSON I CALLED Caroline and when she answered she gave me a mock scolding, "Where have you been? Have you called your mom yet?"

"Yes mom knows I am still alive. You know it is wide open out here and towns are few and far between. Hey listen can you ship my tent to the post office in Williston, North Dakota care of general delivery?" General delivery meant that you walked into the post office, showed your identification, and they gave you your package. I had been camping under a rain fly. It kept me dry but it didn't keep the mosquitos out and they were getting worse by the day. If she got it in the mail soon it would reach Williston before I got there. If not, I would have to wait on it or have to have it forwarded on to Minot, 125 miles even farther down the road.

"That's it? You want me to ship your tent?" she said incredulously.

"Yes please. Mom and dad are on vacation. Do you have a key to the house?"

"Actually I don't"

"I will let the neighbors know that you are going to pick up a key," I explained.

"Okie dokie. When do you need it?"

"Well if you don't get it in the mail pretty quickly, I could possibly pass it up. Can you do it tomorrow?"

She gave a disappointed, "Sure", as if it was the only reason I called.

There was silence on the phone then Caroline sounded hopeful, "By the way, I was with your friends Carlos and Brodie last week!"

"Oh that's nice."

"They miss you!"

"Tell them hello for me."

Another disappointed "OK" came from the other end.

Then a hopeful, "Hey...you *are* coming back to school aren't you?"

"Why do you ask?"

She seemed to be changing subjects and cheerfully said, "You know I spoke with Professor Phelps when I got back home!?"

"And?" I asked.

"Well...word on the street...is that you aren't returning to school?"

Professor Phelps was the most gregarious teacher we had. He knew me quite well and sometimes purposefully and deliberately called me out in class.

But I had never betrayed my deep personal feelings with him, especially not anything about the misgivings I had about my choice of academic path.

"The rumor is that you might have competing interests and that you won't be here in the fall, at last not in any of our classes," she blurted out quickly.

I quickly changed the subject and then said, "Will call again soon! Please get the tent in the mail as quickly as you can. Thanks! Have a good week!"

Montana: Big Sky Country

Newcastle, England

There is a light at the end of the tunnel. No wait that was just an oncoming train.

MINE AND CAROLINE'S RELATIONSHIP would eventually fail but I did graduate from vet school two years later and started work in the stockyards as a contract veterinary epidemiologist for the US Department of Agriculture's "Federal Brucellosis Eradication Program." It was my chance to work in the public health arena and my time with JJ on that Montana ranch may have helped seal the deal on my decision to return to school. I was really what you might call a "disease surveillance specialist" and was paid one whole dollar and fifty cents for every blood sample I drew. The federal government was intent on wiping out bovine brucellosis for good. That is a hard thing to do but they came close before the program costs were transferred to the farmer due to funding cuts. If they didn't entirely eradicate the disease in the United States they gave a good effort. The problem is that the disease could pop up in wildlife herds of bison out west, especially around Yellowstone National Park, and which might come into contact with free ranging domesticated cattle. And then the cycle might continue due to this wildlife reservoir of infection.

Working the stockyards where cattle are bought and sold was the most fun job I have ever had. Sale day was a whirlwind of activity. We had less than 60 seconds to draw the sample before the next cow ran into the chute. On hot summer days, I soaked in sweat and lost a few pounds. I felt like I was part of a large cause. There was a sense of mission - as close as I would ever come to what might be akin to how it was for the World War II generation. Some days we tested over 900 cattle. Other days, when beef prices fell due to drought or from a public relations issue such as "Mad Cow Disease", the number of cattle coming through might fall below 100.

When the program ran dry and all federal funds were cut for contract epidemiologists (I assume $1.50 per blood sample was too high of a cost to survey for a disease that had been nearly wiped out), the US Department of Agriculture sent me to the United Kingdom to help fight the outbreak of a vesicular disease that wreaks havoc on the food supply. The disease is a virus that was spreading through the sheep herds of Great Britain like wildfire. In fact, a similar operational infrastructure established by the US Forest Service in containing wildfires was used by the epidemiologists overseeing the enormous amount of resources that were pouring into Great Britain. There was a sense of mission much like the stockyard program in the U.S. The difference is that there was a greater sense of urgency. Brucellosis is a slow moving, blood borne, bacterial disease, mostly among young heifers. Here, the virus could even be spread from a vehicle driving from one contaminated farm to another and whole farms were being eradicated. People were losing their livelihoods and to make matters worse, the people were basically being quarantined on their own farms. They had sheep dogs that "lost their job" and didn't know what to do with themselves. At times, I felt more like a grievance counselor than a surveillance specialist because I often became the only social contact that they might have due to the quarantine status that was imposed upon them.

As soon as I arrived I was put on what they call "Hot Patrols." Hot patrols are done within 3 kilometers of an infected premise to check for spread to nearby farms. "Surveillance" is done outside the 3 kilometer circle of an infected premise but inside a 10 kilometer circle. I had flown into London on August 23rd (2001) - 6 months after the epidemic had begun. I had a debriefing the next day, and then was sent to Newcastle-upon-Tyne on the following morning's train. The first day in Newcastle I had listened to lectures on protocols all morning, and by the first afternoon had my vehicle stocked with supplies for the next day's farm inspections. Things moved fast and conditions were constantly changing.

Each day I reported to "Allocations" at the Disease Emergency Control Center, a.k.a. "The Deck" (DECC). The Deck provided oversight and coordination for all the data coming in from the field. There were trailers for extra office space for all the different personnel. Some had come in from places like Australia and Germany and had been there since the disease broke in February. Those "veterans" had been moved up to Team Leader. New maps, with overlapping hot patrol and surveillance circles due to multiple infected sites, were created and posted on the wall every morning. A paper sign on the wall had the hand written notice that said, "Hot Patrols clarify instructions for your work with team leaders before going out. ALL COMPLETED PAPERWORK MUST BE RETURNED TO TEAM LEADERS (NOT ALLOCATIONS) FOR AUDITING."

My days usually revolved around the vicinity of the Town of Haydon Bridge, about a 40 minute drive to the west of Newcastle on the A69. Haydon Bridge, which is named after the existing pedestrian bridge across a fork of the Tyne River, is near the ruins of Hadrian's Wall. Even the mighty Roman Empire couldn't handle the feisty Scottish and to keep them out, built the wall across the island of what is now present day Great Britain along the shortest distance possible: between the North Sea, to the west, and the Irish Sea, to the east. It was the most northern extent the Roman Empire would ever reach. On my daily duties, I came across remnants of this wall that was built about 100 years after the birth of Christ by the Roman Emperor after which the wall is named. There are still archeological remains of fortifications in one or two spots along its 73-mile stretch. However, at least in the area of Haydon Bridge, much of it had been pillaged to build Langley Castle during the 14th century, and over the years, farmers had slowly picked it clean to cordon pastureland for their sheep herds. The contemporary political boundary between England and Scotland still roughly follows the old wall.

The best food I could find was in Haydon Bridge at a pub called the General Havelock. I got tired of the standard fish and chips at many restaurants. The General Havelock had a variety of choices from the European menu. Some days the special would be Toulouse sausage with a bean sauce and other days it might be pasta with tomato and basil lamb sauce. The British language was another thing to adjust to. Sometimes someone would hang up the phone at The Deck and say, "He must have been Posh British," meaning "high class." The most famous saying, of which you can buy refrigerator magnets with it written, is the announcement on the London Tube "Mind the gap." The command is implicating you to be careful of the narrow space between the platform and the train. A sign on the Newcastle subway might say, "Always have your ticket with you *whilst* traveling." Or a sign might say, "Enter and *alight* quickly." I assumed that meant to get somewhere and hold on! The exit sign had an arrow and the words, "Way Out." Someone might say, "It'll cost you about 50 quid." One quid is one British Pound. And to "queue up" means to stand in line. People would respond quicker if you asked where the "loo" is instead of the "bathroom."

One morning a farmer named Mr. Cunningham called me and said, "Can you be here at half eight." That meant eight-thirty. It was my second visit to Mr. Cunningham's farm. When I arrived, he said, "You know Miss Dot here can do the work for us." Dot was his Border collie. I had seen these dogs work before and they were astounding. It meant that I wouldn't have to even cross the gate – no biosecurity risk and no scrub down, just look over the 4-foot stone wall from the roadside. The first visit required a hands-on look and examination of a sample of the herd that would give us a statistical probability of whether or not the disease was present. If there were 50 sheep in the herd, then all fifty would have to be examined. But if there were 500 sheep in the herd, according to the statistical calculations, I would only have to examine 93. On the next visit, it was possible to just observe the herd's behavior. If there were any that seemed to be depressed or if there were any that were limping, then the whole examination would have to be completed again.

As I looked over the wall, I saw no sheep anywhere in the vicinity whatsoever. "You mean Dot can corral them into this area beside the road."

"For sure."

"How is she going to get them through that small opening over there that connects to the wide-open back fields?"

"She will slow down and carefully tend to them."

"Sounds good to me!"

Mr. Cunningham stood at the wall with me, whistled, and off Dot disappeared into the back fields. There was a hedge of trees in front of a gentle knoll beyond the corral area that blocked our view of where Dot had gone. The corral area was an open grassy field about the size of a soccer field. The hedge of trees slowly bent towards the wall farther down the line of stone to eventually contain the field on three sides. Mr. Cunningham had placed a small wire fence from the wall where we were standing straight to the hedge of trees to complete the containment of the field on four sides. About 8 minutes later, a few sheep poked their heads through the small opening into the field. We could now see Dot crouched down and moving from side to side according to the different pitches of Mr. Cunningham's whistles. It was as though Mr. Cunningham was moving Dot with an invisible hand. Dot's reactions to the whistles were instantaneous. I held my breath - one wrong move and they would scatter in chaos. At Dot's gentle persuasion, they slowly and patiently moved in a tight group - as one body with many legs. It was one of the most extraordinary events that I have ever witnessed. As they walked across me from left to right, I singled out individual animals – like a wolf would to see which one is vulnerable. My job was to detect any hint of drooping heads, salivation, or lameness. Mr. Cunningham told Dot, "That'll do." And she stopped and fell to her chest with her head up and front legs forward. This allowed them to relax and be in a less heightened state so that we could detect any abnormalities. Mr. Cunningham and I both agreed the herd looked healthy and with the extraordinary help from Dot, I was able to be ahead of schedule for the day's events.

One day out in the field, I was about to walk on a farmer's premise when I got a call from Phil Kophaus in Allocations. It was the first time I had ever used a mobile phone.

"Hey John, this is Phil. Have you scrubbed down yet?"

"Yes sir."

"Have you entered onto the premise?"

"Not yet."

"Good. You are still clean and will be allowed to continue to patrol. Please go to Hunter Oak Farm and get a report in by this evening."

"Yes sir, will do."

Phil was my team leader and was a dairy veterinarian from New Zealand and had been working on the epidemic since nearly the beginning. He must have gotten information that the farm I was about to enter might be infected already due to a neighboring infection. After I had been there a week, he had

OK'd me to have a day off. It couldn't have come at a better time. The morning before my off day I had been on an infected farm and, even though we scrubbed our clothes down before and after leaving any farm, whether infected or not, you were strictly prohibited from visiting another farm for 72 hours after being on an infected premise. If I had not had a day off, I would have been moved from hot patrol to "cull assignment" and may have never gotten back to patrolling clean farms. In some eyes at Allocations I was just a worker bee to be used anyway they saw fit. But to Phil I could sit in the office and do paperwork for a day during my 72 hour quarantine because he valued me more as a surveillance specialist than anything else. Thankfully I would be able to continue patrols with the farmers I had already established a relationship.

A sign had been put up at HQ that summed up the chaotic atmosphere. "There is a light at the end of the tunnel. No wait that was just an oncoming train." I had three American colleagues that had been in London with me from the beginning. Amadi and Gavin were from Colorado and Anna was from rural South Georgia. This was Amadi's second tour and he helped us navigate the bureaucracy and politics of DEFRA – Department of Environment, Farms, and Rural Affairs, an agency beneath the Ministry of Agriculture, Fisheries, and Food- the United Kingdom's equivalent of the US Department of Agriculture. We were brought into the epidemic near the end and there was a lot of frustration in getting the disease completely eradicated. Rumors were flying around about where the disease had started 6 months earlier, if it was a hoax, and why the higher ups weren't allowing vaccination. We know it wasn't a hoax - there had been virus isolation in the laboratory - but the answers to the other questions were very complex. Nonetheless, people were getting very weary.

On the afternoon of September 11, 2001, Gavin called me to ask if I had heard the news. The UK is 7 hours ahead of the Eastern Time Zone. "I have been away from the phone all morning inspecting sheep at Brokenheugh," I replied. Greg said, "Well turn on the TV when you get back to the hotel. Something with terrorists has happened back home." I thought to myself, "Just another silly scare." Little did I know the horrific events that were unfolding. The Brokenheugh Farm overlooked Hayden Bridge and was right in the middle of a hot spot. I had a double weight of sadness. The next day, the farmers that I had come to know were telling me how sorry they felt for America's loss and yet they were losing everything about their livelihoods. There was dual consoling. I would say, "Thank you. But your suffering is no less, just under different circumstances."

I was now juggling about 7 different clean farms for follow-up visits on 2-3 day intervals to recheck for presence of disease. On September 16, 2001, I did the final inspection of Mr. Cunningham's small farm. He had been caught inside the 3 kilometer hot zone but it had been 21 days since the initial visit. I was responsible for his farm from start to finish and he was now completely cleared of disease. We contemplated for about an hour while looking over the stone wall at his sheep. Mr. Oaks of Hunter Oak Farm drove up and joined us. He started talking about American beer and said, "I've seen lemonade darker." Mr. Cunningham chimed in, "Hard to get pissed (drunk) isn't it?" Whereby Mr. Oaks responded, "I guess you can, it just takes a bit o' work."

The last confirmed case occurred on September 30, 2001.[13] The U.S. was pulling us out and not sending in anyone else due to the events of 9-11. My tour would officially be over on the first day that planes resumed flights across the Atlantic. I got on a 747 to Washington, D.C. on September 22, 2001. The plane was enormous yet so empty that it seemed like you could have played catch with a baseball. I laid the armrests down on the 7 or 8 seats in the middle row and took a nap.

BY THE TIME I reached North Dakota, it was impossible to eat breakfast in camp due to the increasing mosquito population. There was a consistent group of about 10 bicyclers heading east. Some were headed to the University of Michigan; one group was going to Montreal; others had itineraries that took them to distant places elsewhere. I only saw them at night; there were few places to camp in the endless grasslands and we all usually found the same place in a small town about 75 miles farther down the road, give or take 5 or 10 miles, from the previous night. Each morning I would pack as fast as possible once I left the safe zone from inside my tent's netting. The swarms of mosquitoes, which consisted of hundreds if not thousands of individuals, would literally, and I really mean literally, drive a person mad. Packing was an event to be done in as few seconds as possible. Don't even think about trying to boil water on the small camp stove that I hauled around to make a cup of coffee at the picnic table. We then rode to the nearest café in the nearest town to get coffee and breakfast inside the safe haven of a building. The breeze created from propelling the bicycle was enough to keep the swarms away.

One morning in the town of Lakota, we stopped at a café that was adjoined to a Chevrolet dealership. Our waitress worked the whole place including the counter where about eight men in overalls were gathered and who appeared like they had sat in that same exact spot every morning for probably decades. The waitress wore a white apron as she hustled around on her chubby short legs and appeared to still have the same hairstyle from when she was a teenager in the 1950's. You had to walk across the showroom floor to get to the bathroom. We looked comically juxtapositioned in this setting that seemed to be frozen in time as we walked in wearing dirty T-shirts and frizzled hair from wearing a bike helmet.

Everyone of course looked up as we entered. They were much too polite to stare. They were very friendly and warm and said, "Good morning!" I don't remember much conversation in the room except among ourselves, and the farmers (I assumed) continued on what they were doing - reading the paper, joking with the waitress, or laughing at each other. When we were done eating, the waitress said, "I will lay your tab down here, take your time. By the way, the coffee is free."

One of the men at the counter had paid for all of our coffee. Which one, I haven't a clue. We would soon be crossing the Minnesota state line and it was a very kind, and at least for us, a ceremonial-like farewell to the 900 mile-crossing of the Great Plains.

Pulled over early in Williston, North Dakota. The strategy was to reach Minot, 125 miles away, in one long day. In Minot, the Northern Lights came out in spectacular fashion. Unfortunately, I was too exhausted to keep my eyes open.

The Detour: Ely, Minnesota

"Moose burger or caribou dog?" - *Northern Exposure*

I HAD FALLEN ABOUT 3000 feet in elevation since leaving Browning, Montana. If you had put a marble on the road to follow us, it would have rolled so slowly that it would probably just be leaving the outskirts of Browning by now. I reached Bagley, Minnesota,on July 18. Bagley is 90 miles east of the North Dakota border and it is roughly where the forest returns. I had spent the previous night in Grand Forks, North Dakota, crossed the Red River at the Minnesota border in the morning, and spent all day getting back to a forested campground for the first time since leaving Glacier National Park. At one point along the Hi-Line I had tallied 473 miles without ever seeing a traffic light. I really, really wanted to see trees again and wasn't going to stop until I found them.

I had crossed the Laurentian Divide and gone back into the Arctic Watershed again somewhere in North Dakota west of Grand Forks, probably around Lakota. The Laurentian Divide dives south out of Canada and makes a long sweeping arc diagonally across North Dakota, reaches all the way down to South Dakota, and runs back up through the farmland of northwestern Minnesota as if to gather in all the tributaries to the Red River like a big hand scooping out a chunk of the US's upper Midwest in one last ditch effort before running back into Canada.

Thus the Red River flows almost due north and this itself creates some interesting phenomena, especially in the form of chronic spring floods. First of all, the river hardly has any slope to it. It could just as easily be considered a very wide drainage pathway in a landscape that is relatively flat all around. In Fargo, North Dakota, to the south but upstream of Grand Forks, the elevation is 904 feet. At Grand Forks, eighty miles to the north but downstream, the elevation has dropped a whopping... 61 feet. That is roughly 1 millimeter of fall every 23 feet. By comparison, on my ride across the Great Plains, I had dropped roughly 1 millimeter every 5 feet on average. The ride across the Great Plains was at least four times steeper than the grade of the Red River! Who would've known the Great Plains to be so slanted? Second, since it is so wide and shallow, the Red River easily freezes over in the winter. To make matters worse, as things begin to thaw in South Dakota from the approaching spring, the river to the north still has ice. The ice creates a dam and things begin to back up. Throw in a warm spell to melt the snow and ice a little faster along with a rain shower in early spring and you have a disaster on hand. The river just oozes out of its banks and across a wide expanse of farmland in the Red River Valley, if you can call it a valley, like a spilt glass of water slowly creeping across a table. In the epic flood of 1997, parts of the Red River Valley had water extending 20 miles wide.[14]

As you cross the Red River into Minnesota, you will see combines gathering corn and soybeans from the fields in late summer and Highway 2 is still a 4-lane rural thoroughfare divided by a wide grassy median and that runs so flat and straight all the way to the horizon that the Jolly Green Giant could use it as a bowling alley. But at Erskine, Minnesota, yet still inside the very edge of the Red River Valley, there sits an oblong-shaped shallow pothole-like body of water less than 1 mile across that is typical of the glacially carved lakes found in the area that were left behind from the previous ice age, of which there are dozens, and is the first indication that we were indeed leaving the Great Plains. It's called Cameron Lake and butts right into town at the end of 1st Street, not 400 feet from US Highway 2, and where I ate lunch at a picnic table across the street from the square, flat roofed, ascetic post office and its customary flag pole, with kids splashing near the beach, and with naturally landscaped trees for the first time in nearly 1000 miles.

From there, we caught a tail-wind because of cold fronts passing through. A glorious tailwind! It almost feels like you are coasting down a hill! The cold fronts periodically showered rain down upon us as they speedily passed by and then the sun would soon reappear. It seemed as if I had peddled across the entire Great Plains with a slight dry breeze in my face. Just enough head wind to irritatingly feel like you were pedaling up a slight incline. So the shift in winds also signified a dramatic change in venue. Then it was jolting to see spruce trees suddenly appear almost from nowhere as we approached Bagley in the waning moments of daylight. It felt as though we had emerged from a cave that had a fog blowing out of it, and when it all cleared, voila! A whole forest of trees, glorious trees!

My main riding partners had been a couple who lived in Banff, Alberta, named Malik and Kala. He was a carpenter and she was a bilingual customer service representative and who were on their way to visit friends and family in Montreal. We first camped together just this side of Browning, Montana, in fact, on my very first night after leaving Glacier National Park. It was a relief to find new companions so quickly. I had lost them when I stopped in Culbertson but caught up with them again in North Dakota. It was uncanny how we knew where each other would be stopping for the night. I guess we all had the same goals and intuitively found the same place– somewhere that is safe, clean, cheap, and has water. A tree or two would be icing on the cake. I always pedaled alone but we often stopped for breakfast together if we could find a café and we found each other again at night. Like birds in flock that come to roost just before the sun goes down.

Cafes were few and far between in the Plains but now the population density was starting to increase – yet another indication of changing conditions. Between Grand Forks and Bagley, we had eaten at a café in Fisher, Minnesota, a tiny town with 435 people and that sits on a bend of the Red *Lake* River, another wide flat-land tributary to the *Red* River.

After leaving Bagley, I got the 1.99 special at a café along the highway one mile east of the tiny town of Wilton, population 204. Wilton is no bigger than most towns I had gone through in the Great Plains but the overall density was increasing as evident by the sprawl – an increasing number of tiny communities scattered along US 2. Paradoxically, in the Great Plains, it was as though the population was at such an irreducible minimum that they could not afford any sprawl and the towns there were more concentrated. Nelson County, North Dakota (Lakota), the one to the west of Grand Forks County and where we ate breakfast in the Chevy dealership, has a population of 2,968 people. Clearwater County, Minnesota (Bagley) is almost identical in land size and has a population that is 3 times larger yet Lakota is only half the size of Bagley. In the Great Plains you had to fill several water bottles at each town in order to traverse the long hot gaps between each one. Here you almost didn't need one. In the Great Plains you had to plan way ahead, study the maps, make sure everything was tuned on the bike, and you still never felt at ease navigating the long distances. For me the preparation and vigilance was intense. I often pedaled all day, fell in the tent with barely any supper, and was soon sound asleep. Up again at sunrise and repeat. But in Bena, Minnesota, population 116, I was able to play the jukebox and drink a beer at lunch for the first time since leaving Glacier National Park.

The Mississippi Headwaters State Forest surrounds the stretch of US 2 between Bagley and Bemidji. Somewhere along that stretch of highway where it had seemed to close-in and narrowed down to a two-lane road bordered by quaking aspen trees, I had finished skirting through a piece of the Arctic Watershed for a second time as I left the Red River Basin. Although the true beginning of the Mississippi River begins as a trickle in Itasca State Park, it begins to pick up enough steam to float a canoe somewhere just south of US Highway 2. The river actually meanders *north* out of Lake Itasca and then begins a broad, slow, patient, 30-mile long sweeping curve to the east before finally turning south while connecting several natural glacial lakes like pearls on a necklace. There are so many that there is more lake than there is river. Kind of like, "Do you want a little spaghetti with that sauce?"

In Bemidji, Minnesota, at the exact spot where the Mississippi River connects two of those clear turquois lakes, Paul Bunyan Drive squeezes between them and bridges a piece of the string that is less than 3 city blocks long and so narrow that an average athlete could long jump across. The bridge is so indistinct that if you stand at the edge of the water underneath you must duck so that you don't hit your head. If I wasn't sure I had made it through the Great Plains, I knew now because there is an 18-foot tall statue of the street's namesake and Babe the Blue Ox in the park around Lake Bemidji, the larger of the two lakes that lies on the north side of the bridge. Kala snapped a picture of me leaning against Babe with my arm stretched out and my hand resting just above her elbow.

The water below the bridge is still flowing north but then the river abruptly dumps out of the east side of Lake Bemidji like the spout on a tea pot while the lake itself continues to expand to the north nearly to the horizon. I had a broken bar on my back rack that needed to be welded and Bemidji was also the first place in two weeks whereby I left US 2 to go into town for errands but re-entered the highway farther east, like when a race car drives through pit row.

But very soon I would be leaving my riding partners for good. The magic of Minnesota has haunted me my whole life. And the town of Ely, Minnesota, had become my ghost house filled with Casper-like spirits. Ely draws me in like The Sirens of Homer's *Odyssey*. I had always worked in Ely anytime I had a break from college up until the moment I pedaled off of the Pacific shoreline of Washington just 4 weeks earlier. Over the past spring I had felt a twinge of betrayal as I planned this quest that I was now on. Ely still today teases me and when the seasons begin to change I wonder are the lakes thawed by now? Or are they thick enough to ski on yet? As my friends were to continue east, I was to detour through the heart of this magnificent land dominated by meandering waterways, bogs, and balsam fir. It is where my second career in environmental science took root. It is where I would later return in my late thirties to gain the education I needed to begin that second career. The day after camping in a birch grove at Deer River, Minnesota, Malik, Kala, and I ate breakfast in the town of Cohasset, where the Mississippi River just begins to toy with the idea of turning south and re-crosses US Highway 2 through marshland filled with Black Spruce and Speckled Alder, and where Tamarack trees grow in the upland edges of the wide swamps surrounding the wild river corridor that is as narrow as the nearby streams that feed it. I broke tradition of riding at my own pace and stayed alongside my companions during that last day together for one final drawn-out farewell. After eating lunch in Grand Rapids, the spot at which the US Army Corps of Engineers put their first dam on the Mississippi and turned it from a frontier waterway into one that was to be tamed by man, I turned north and left US Hwy 2 for much longer than just running errands.

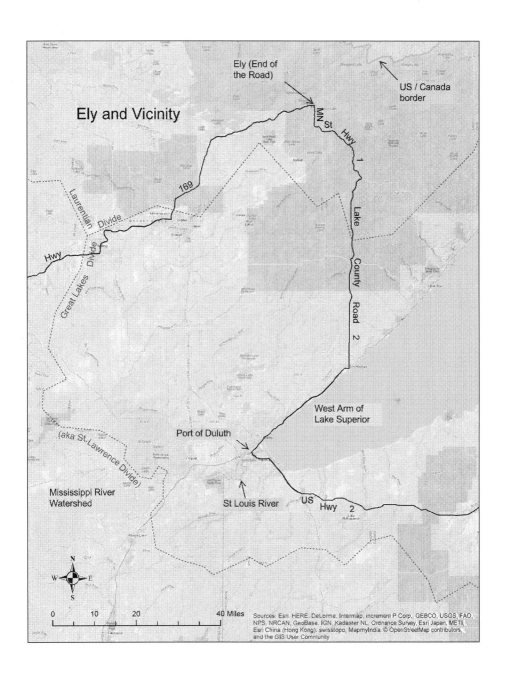

Ely (End of the Road)

US / Canada border

Ely and Vicinity

MN St Hwy 1

169

Laurentian Divide

Great Lakes Divide

Hwy

Lake County Road 2

West Arm of Lake Superior

Port of Duluth

(aka St Lawrence Divide)

Mississippi River Watershed

St Louis River

US Hwy 2

N
W   E
S

0   10   20   40 Miles

Sources: Esri, HERE, DeLorme, Intermap, increment P Corp., GEBCO, USGS, FAO, NPS, NRCAN, GeoBase, IGN, Kadaster NL, Ordnance Survey, Esri Japan, METI, Esri China (Hong Kong), swisstopo, MapmyIndia, © OpenStreetMap contributors, and the GIS User Community

And for the second time, I waved goodbye to closely bonded friends that I have never seen again.

ELY, MINNESOTA, IS ANOTHER one of the few places in the Continental US where the water flows neither to the Pacific Ocean, the Mississippi River, the Atlantic Ocean, nor the Gulf of Mexico. Somewhere along Highway 169 just north of the town of Virginia, Minnesota, I climbed two miles to get over a 400-foot high hump where the Laurentian Divide stays close to the border but wiggles back inside the US; I had fallen into the Arctic Watershed...again... for the third time. Ely is called the Far Northland for good reason. It is 300 miles farther north than Toronto and 30 miles more north than the tip top of Maine. For example, as part of a publicity stunt for tourism development, one year the Ely Chamber of Commerce announced that Canada had attempted to annex Ely in the April fool's Day edition of the local newspaper. The paper did their journalistic duty and reported both sides of the issue; some locals were as indignant as cats that had been put in water and others couldn't wait to leave the Union.

Ely began as a mining town to exploit the valuable iron ore discovered there at the end of the American Civil War. It is located on the southern edge of the boreal forest - the forest that encircles the top of the globe just below the Arctic Circle. It is the last stand of trees before the Earth's landscape turns to tundra, a scrubby, treeless area where the polar bears roam. The boreal forest canopy is dominated by balsam fir and spruce trees. If you could ride in a spaceship and look down on the top of the globe during the winter time, you would see this forest around the upper latitudes as a narrow band of greenery poking up through the white-out like a Christmas wreath had been laid on the top of the earth. Thus Ely morphed into a logging town to harvest this other valuable natural resource after the mines had become unprofitable due to depletion of the richest veins and from global competition. Although logging still occurs today, mostly through managed plantations by the US Forest Service, Ely primarily has now settled into being the gateway to the Canoe Capital of the World. There are 2 million acres of roadless wilderness with thousands of pristine lakes, portage trails, wetlands, and streams all meandering northward towards Lake Winnipeg, the "sixth Great Lake," the same destination as the Red River.

This huge expanse of managed wilderness incorporates the invisible border between the US and Canada and is equally divided on either side. In this part of the North American Continent, the border between the two countries follows the traditional navigable waterway that was the most direct route into the interior of the continent from Lake Superior and that was most often used by the French-Canadian paddlers who traded for furs with the Algonquin indigenous people. It was an amicable relationship-so much so that many of the traders married into the tribes. Some may argue that they only did it to gain favor with the tribes and push out competing traders. Nonetheless, these 18th century European entrepreneurs had no interest to settle the land and extract it from the native people. And that kept the peace, if not between competing Europeans, at least between the two cultures. If you paddle into this public area still today, it is as remote and pristine as the day the first Voyageur out of Montreal entered this treasure trove of natural resources. In fact, some Ojibwa tribes use the area for sustenance hunting and fishing still today. The water is as clean as any on the planet. It always seemed silly to me that border regulations even existed but I guess every bureaucracy has to protect its turf. The better solution, it seems to me, would be to draw a circle around the 2 million acres lying in both countries and have controlled access by an international police force that consisted of US agents on the US side and Canadian agents on the Canadian side. Instead of the point of regulation occurring at the political line that splits the wilderness in half, the point of regulation would occur at the perimeter. Both countries would be in constant communication and everyone wins: increased efficiency for both governments, less hassle to the wilderness visitor, and increased security for both countries.

There are only three national high adventure programs run by the Boys Scouts of America's home office in Irving, Texas, and one is located in Ely. In the summer I was a "Charlie Guide" (there are women guides too; the term is named after an early founder from 1923) at the Northern Tier High Adventure Base and took groups of 8 on backcountry fishing and canoeing adventures. In the winter we ran a program called "Okpik"[15] from the day after Christmas through February, where kids would pull sleds with cross-country skis, or ride behind sled dogs, and camp out in polar domes that were made from hollowed out piles of snow. In January you can ski across the same lake that you paddled across in June. The director liked to say, "You know, the temperature in Celsius and the temperature in Fahrenheit is the same at minus 40." Diving into one of those crisp lakes whose surface is reflective enough to recognize your own face blemishes on a still hot July day is as much relief as a cool breeze on a cloudless day in the Arizona desert. Yet the lakes of the Canoe Capital of the World became perfectly flat white football fields after Thanksgiving. In fact, if you want to traverse from Ely into Canada, the *only* way is by canoe or on skis.

During the one week I was off the bike and volunteered at The Base, I took one day to get out to the North Hegman Lake pictographs. Northern Tier is located on Moose Lake and being only six miles via continuous waterway to the Canadian ranger station at Prairie Portage, it just wasn't that convenient to get over to the Hegman Lake area. I had never seen probably the most visited and arguably best set of pictographs in the Boundary Waters / Quetico Wilderness. It is a free outdoor art gallery – no membership required. Fortunately, they are accessible via a dirt road out from Ely, two short portages, and two short paddles. The pictographs were drawn with red paint most likely made from iron-ore, among other things, out of the very rocks they were painted on by an Ojibwa artist many centuries ago. The paintings are on a flat rock the size of an interstate billboard and that overhangs the shoreline in one corner of the lake. Here is my attempt at an interpretation:

They are of a human with long outstretched arms and hands the size of basketballs, possibly symbolizing a spiritual character; a dog or wolf with a very long tail, possibly being a caricature of the animal; and a detailed depiction of a bull moose without any exaggerations and with an impressive rack of antlers. The "spirit" character is not stick-like but it is not detailed either, there being no discernable eyes, hair, or ears. The body tapers uniformly, almost wedge-like, from the chest to the legs. Below these three is a horizontal line with a slight dip in it that may symbolize the earth on which the two animals are standing upon, with the spirit character being slightly above them. The animals are correctly proportioned to each other while the spirit character is nearly double the size of the moose. To the right of the head of the spirit character appears to be a small school of fish. And above the spirit character are three rudimentary canoes - a single curved lined representing each one - two of them with very small blocky stick-like figures.

After the week of visiting old friends, I was ready to move on through my 200-mile detour. I rode due east early one morning on the only other paved exit out of Ely – MN State Hwy 1. After a while I turned right onto Lake County Road 2 and rode it through Superior National Forest all the way to the shore of Lake Superior at which I entered the small town of Two Harbors - the only sign of civilization since leaving Ely. I made another right turn at Two Harbors and rode the shoreline all the way to the port of Duluth. On my way to Duluth that day, I finally left the Arctic Watershed for good because somewhere along the road to Two Harbors I had crossed into my fourth major continental watershed and gone over the Great Lakes Divide.

Lake Superior is considered an inland fresh water sea. It drains east through all the other Great Lakes and its water eventually reaches the Atlantic

Ocean via the St. Lawrence River. It takes an average drop of water 321 years to do that.[16] Lake Superior could hold the water of all the other Great Lakes combined and contains 10% of the world's surface fresh water that isn't frozen. It has a surface area of 31,700 square miles, an average depth of 483 feet, and can have hurricane-like waves on a treacherous day. Gordon Lightfoot makes this vividly clear in his tragic song *The Edmond Fitzgerald*. Approaching Lake Superior, it is so enormous that it becomes indistinguishable where the sky ends and the lake begins; they appear to blend together as one. The rural road into Two Harbors sits up high above the Lake on a plateau and so, on a clear day, you feel as though - if not for the white birch and quaking aspen trees - you might be flying in the sky itself because the blue surface of the Lake sits just below your line of site and the sky just above.

Large bodies of water such as Lake Superior are heat capacitors; they store heat in the summer and release heat in the winter. Therefore they moderate the local climate. Ely is far enough inland from the Lake that it can be as much as 10 degrees colder in the winter and 10 degrees hotter in the summer as compared to Two Harbors or Duluth. When I left Ely I was in short sleeve shirt on this clear summer day. Even before the Lake became visible, I could feel the temperature dropping and by the time I was within 3 miles of the shore, I had stopped already to put on a fleece.

YEARS LATER WHEN I was living in Ely, I realized that you couldn't get through the winter without consuming high density food and lots of it. It took almost too many calories to survive the day after day of below freezing temperatures.

I decided that I would buy a rifle and acquire a deer hunting license well before the fall hunting season. In Ely, even on a sweltering 80 degree day in July, you were always planning for winter. "Do I have enough birch stockpiled for the wood burning stove?" Now that meant, "Do I have enough stockpiled *12 months in advance* because the split wood that was dumped in your driveway or front yard was cut from a live stock of birch or green ash, the most calorie dense wood that burned the hottest. But only if it was dry. Thus the 12-month "seasoning" process for the wood was required in order to keep a house warm when it was 25 degrees below zero many nights. Otherwise the heat from the stove was wasted just dehydrating wood and not heating the house sufficiently. In the summer time, you might be thinking you had enough wood for *this* winter but you were also thinking about the winter beyond as well.

So I started wondering if I had enough meat to get me through the upcoming winter. I drove to the town of Virginia and found a nice used Winchester 30-30 for 200 bucks. It took me about 20 minutes to decide. "I'll take it." I had to submit a background check and 3 days later I was back in Virginia to pick up the rifle.

"Need a scope?" the clerk asked.

"No sir but I'll take a 20-box of ammunition."

I then went to the hardware store in Ely and figured out the nuances of the current year's hunting regulations. They are always based on what zone you wanted to hunt and on what the deer mortality surveys found in the previous spring. I had worked one of the deer mortality transects for the Minnesota Department of Natural Resources. You basically have a one-mile compass bearing you walk through a wooded area on public lands. You record any deer carcasses you find and how the site looked. Was it killed by wolves or did it starve? If they weren't killed by wolves, which most aren't because a wolf chase is only successful in about 1 out of every 7 attempts, then they usually died from starvation in early spring. By April, if a deer hadn't quite put enough fat stores away in the previous leaf season, he is out of gas. When your car is out of gas, you pull over and walk to a gas station to fill a gas can so you can start it again. When a deer is out of gas, it dies. A deer with depleted fat stores in the bone marrow would have died from starvation. Sometimes these bones are left after a wolf kill and can be examined. Fat stores usually means wolf kill, no fat stores usually means starvation. If most of the deer died by starvation then the hunting quota gets reduced. If killed by a wolf, it doesn't affect the hunting quota with much significance. The reason is because long hard winters have a much larger effect on deer populations than wolf kills. Deer populations that are hammered by hard winters fall dramatically and then recover over a few years' time. Wolf kills are a near constant. And wolf populations are dependent on deer populations, not the other way around. In other words, the local wolf population would go extinct long before the deer population fell to any threatening level. It takes about 5 times more deer than wolves to sustain one wolf family. If the deer population falls below the 5 times multiplier, the wolf population reaches a tipping point at which it cannot sustain itself and would eventually decline to zero. It's a basic ecological principle that energy flows from the bottom up and not the other way around.

I bought a license in a nearby hunting zone that allowed the taking of both does and bucks with a rifle. Besides, I had a friend who owned a home in the same zone and was at his house on the first day of hunting season. Fortunately, my friend was in South America visiting his girlfriend and he needed a house sitter. His house happened to be out on a wooded tract of land and well outside the town limits. I got up before dawn and made a pot of coffee. It was already below freezing in the early twilight of late November. After having my coffee and watching the sun slowly creep above the horizon, I sat in a chair on the gravel driveway that faced a wooded field on a power line about 75 yards away. I thought to myself, "That has to be a good place for deer to wander into and it also gives me a good line of site." I sat for about an hour and then got impatient. So I walked back inside to get another cup of coffee. When I came back to the door, there was a big doe standing on the power line. I leaned against the door frame…Slowly put the gun up to my shoulder…Looked down the barrel, sited on the deer's chest…And pulled the trigger.

It bolted! "Did I miss!?" I ran to the power line where it had been standing and carried the rifle with me. It was loaded with two more bullets. At the edge of the woods next to the field, I saw bright red blood on a birch sapling. I followed it to another sapling with a blood splotch and continued on for another 25 yards. Then there it lay. I let out a sigh of relief, "I don't have to shoot it again." It was dead. I had never fired the gun before and have never fired the gun since, not even to site test it on a firing range. And I swear on the Bible that the box of ammunition still sits in my underwear drawer today with 19 bullets in it.

THAT WINTER IN ELY I had 60 pounds of boneless meat in my freezer. I had hamburger, steaks, and roasts. At Christmas I made jerky and gave some away as gifts. But I thought it was ridiculous to have a freezer running in the house when it never got above freezing outside for at least 3 months during the year. So I eventually decided to pack everything in a wood box and set it in a snowbank by the side door to the driveway. I wasn't worried about people stealing my winter stores but the perennial wintertime resident of Ely, the Raven, was probably the only thing that would have enough intelligence to find a way to open the lid so that he could cache it away for himself and the only one with enough curiosity to want to know what's inside. I secured the lid to the box and turned the freezer off.

I estimated the doe to be about 200 pounds on the hoof. In Florida, that would be a huge deer but for the cold climate of northern Minnesota it is only average. The farther north you go in the northern hemisphere, the larger the deer get. It is another ecological principle that has to do with heat conservation; the larger you are the less surface area (skin) there is to lose heat in proportions to your overall body mass. For example, the inside of golf ball could hold about

41 milliliters of water and has 11 square inches of covering. A basketball could hold 180 times more water than a golf ball but only needs about 25 times more covering than a golf ball does. If you were to heat the water before you put it in each ball, the water inside would eventually cool down to room temperature; the water in the golf ball would reach room temperature significantly quicker though.

So you might ask, "Well how in the world do tiny Chickadees, which don't migrate, survive a boreal winter?" They have other winter time adaptations, such as the ability to go into hibernation mode at night, whereby metabolism slows down and energy is conserved. But what's interesting is that the Black Capped Chickadee, the northern version, is about 10% bigger than a Carolina Chickadee, the southern version. Elevation is analogous to moving north climatically speaking, and so biologists have even determined at what elevation in the Great Smoky Mountains National Park separates the two chickadee species.[17] This delineating elevation line was roughly at 4000 feet in 1952. I could imagine this delineating line migrating upwards until the black capped chickadee has been squeezed out of the Smokey Mountains.

IF YOU GO TO the International Wolf Center in Ely, Minnesota, you will see a stuffed wolf on display that has been commemorated: Wolf 919, a 75 pound male that lived to be at least 6 years old but no more than 10 years old. No matter how old he lived he got to pass on his genes to the next generation and he certainly beat the odds. The average life span of a wolf in the wild is 4 years. He was scrappy and a survivor. I know because I tracked him during the winter months of early 2008. One day during the third week of March, I placed the telemetry device down on the Wolf Center Director's desk and said,

"Found him."

"You did!?"

"Without a doubt. Clear strong signal. The hard part was getting a triangulation."

"Why, where were you?"

"All the way to Twin Lakes. Unplowed!"

We had gotten a 6-inch dump the night before. The major thoroughfares usually get plowed immediately, sometimes even in the middle of the night. When exactly they get plowed depends on the amount of snowfall, the forecast, and available resources from the state. Some local roads get plowed by the municipality or sometimes a local resident will have a plow on front of his or her truck. The Twin Lakes Road has few residents and sometimes the road may go a week without getting plowed.

Wolf 919 had been collared by the US Geological Survey when he was a juvenile with his home pack. But the USGS had run out of funding and he had not been tracked regularly on the ground in 3 years. Every once in a while they would send a plane up to log a position on the wolves that had been collared or check for a mortality signal – if the collar doesn't move for 24 hours, it will automatically send a steady ping that is distinctly different than the normal transmission that comes from a live wolf. GPS collars were still too expensive and the cost could not be justified at the time 919 had been trapped. In the meantime, it was known that he had left his home pack, found a female, and was well on his way to forming a new pack. The Wolf Center in conjunction with Vermilion College, the local community college, had taken over duties in order to determine the boundaries of his territory. We had gotten about a dozen locations on him at different times of the day but we needed at least 30 to be confident in drawing an accurate polygon. We had a rough idea of what the borders might be due to the information we had on nearby packs; wolves from one pack do not let wolves from another pack come into their territory. And we had information according to other constraints such as roads, which often create pack borders. But we had never expected him to be as far west as Twin Lakes. It had been almost 2 weeks since we last got a reading on him. I had gone down the Twin Lakes Road almost in desperation.

"Yeah, I had to drive straight-in all the way to the lake without turning the wheels too much." The director looked puzzled. I owned a manual transmission front wheel drive Mazda Protégé. It was nearly foolish to do what I had done. I figured that I would be walking the two miles back to the main highway.

"I got the first signal standing on the lake. He was real close. Must have been on the lake somewhere."

The director just looked at me and nodded.

If you are not familiar with Ely, Minnesota, the lakes stay frozen thick enough to drive a tractor trailer on until May. In fact, the town actually plows a "road", with light posts and all, across Shagawa Lake every winter. Everyone, including school buses, use it to cut the corner when going from the northern "suburbs" into town. The word *suburb* is used lightly because Ely is smack-dab in the middle of the wilderness. Ely is so remote that the "End of the Road Radio" (WELY AM 1450 / FM 94.5) is one of the few radio stations left in the US that are mandated by the FCC to provide official emergency information to local residents in times of crises.

I continued on, "Then I put it in reverse and drove backwards until I got to where West Boundary Road forks west. I stopped the car, put the emergency brake on, and walked down West Boundary about 50 yards to get the second signal. Not the best triangulation, but it worked."

When you use telemetry, one signal cannot pinpoint where your subject is. He is obviously somewhere on the line of the signal, but where on the line? So you have to move away, preferably as perpendicular to the line of the first signal as much as possible. You record the compass direction of the two signals, draw them on a map, and where they cross is your location point. I got back in the car after getting the second signal, held the driver door open, slowly released the clutch, held my head out the door looking backwards, and steered the car in reverse. I figured I would go as far as I could and then start walking. I could hardly believe it when I finally saw the dark, plowed pavement of the main highway. I had made it!

I loved the winters that I spent in Ely. The cold air was crisp and clean. Noise was muffled and it seemed as quiet as a library. You never had to worry about being wet - everything was frozen. I would build up so much heat cross-country skiing across a lake that I would begin shedding layers until I was in a T-shirt, and although the wind was blowing across my hands, I could hold my ski poles with no gloves. In early spring when the lakes were still frozen and the temperatures would rise above freezing, sled dogs couldn't run quite so fast due to heat exhaustion. I think that if scientists said that we were in a dramatic global cooling down period, there would be mass panic. There is a cartoon posted on my home office wall that I clipped from Cartoon Parade. It shows two guys looking out an office window at a massive ice sheet. The caption says, "A looming glacier certainly puts things into perspective." So where is the science in our public policies? Well it gets there eventually - usually it takes years or even decades. But it does get there. The director of the Wolf Center one day told me, "You know John, politics trumps science." This was coming from a scientist that was a small part of the decades-long research that eventually changed people's view of how predators interact with the ecosystem. The work changed public opinion so much so that the wolf has been brought back from the brink of extinction in the Upper Midwest. The biggest threat to the wolf in Ely now is being hit by a car. This viewpoint coming from the director might be a little too cynical but the point was well made. I don't ever expect policy to *not* be influenced by politics. It's just that today, the political rhetoric seems to have skewed things a bit too much.

WHILE I WAS IN Ely and working at the International Wolf Center, I had also been working and taking classes in ecology at Vermilion College. The two institutions collaborated and shared resources and one of my jobs was to paddle out and retrieve the telemetry collar from wolves that had died. We would get general coordinates from the plane as to its general location. According to how far they were in the wilderness, sometimes we could paddle out, hopefully find it along the closest portage trail with the telemetry equipment, and get back home in a day. At other times, it would be so far out that it was impossible to paddle there, retrieve it, and get back home before dark and so we had to camp overnight. Once you got within 50 meters of the deceased wolf, the telemetry would ping clearly in almost any direction and you couldn't tell which way to walk. And the dead wolf might be hidden among the thick underbrush. Usually when you got real close though, Turkey Vultures would fly up and revealed the secret spot.

Another of my projects was to re-start the Superior National Forest's Boreal Owl study. The biologist who had designed the study, and who five years earlier had put up 100 nesting boxes on the trunks of White Spruce or Balsam Fir trees about 20 feet above the ground, had not been able to monitor them in the past 2 years. So I was given the coordinates of all the boxes and was directed to check each one during the nesting season in the first week of May and then write a report.

Boreal Owls don't build their own nests and therefore utilize natural holes in trees or ones that had been carved by woodpeckers. Nesting boxes were a good substitute, kind of like putting up a Bluebird box, and you could place them randomly throughout the forest. The boxes weren't that big because the Boreal Owl is no bigger than a Robin. The Boreal Owl was a species of concern due to possibly declining populations and so we wanted to see if we could figure out what kind of habitat they preferred in which to nest. It helps inform managers of the Superior National Forest how to balance the competing demands between commercial logging permits and forest conservation. The problem is that in the three years they had been monitored, a similar species that seems to be doing OK, the Northern Saw-whet Owl, had always been found in any occupied box and not one Boreal Owl had ever been seen using them. And there were never many that were occupied in the first place. Therefore data was severely lacking to inform any conclusion. When I checked them, seven of the boxes had been severely damaged or were lying on the ground. Of the ninety-three left, five had been used.

One day I called Dave, the national forest biologist, and said, "There is a Boreal Owl in number seventy-three."

He said, "Really?! Are you sure?"

I replied, "Yeah, it has the right markings. Please go verify."

A day later he called back, "Yep, it's definitely a Boreal."

About two days after that I called again, "There is a Boreal Owl in number twelve."

He hadn't known me very well and still wasn't 100% confident in my ability to distinguish it from the Northern Saw-whet Owl. "Please go verify," I said.

The next day he affirmed, "Wow! It's a Boreal."

Same lake along the Minnesota-Ontario border:

January

June

The Great Lakes Watershed

"Toto, I've a feeling we're not in Kansas anymore." – Dorothy, *The Wizard of Oz*

LAKE SUPERIOR'S ELEVATION AT full pool is 600 feet above sea level. It drains into Lake Huron, elevation 577 feet, via the St Marys River. Lake Huron in turn drains into Lake Erie, elevation 569, via the Detroit River. It then drains into Lake Ontario, elevation 243 feet, via Niagara Falls. The interesting thing is that Ely is only 48 miles from the shore of Lake Superior as the crow flies but Lake Superior does not capture any of its water. In some areas around Lake Michigan, the area of drainage from the shoreline only extends outward across the land for a mere 9 miles. Along the shoreline that I rode to Duluth, there are majestic cliffs 100 feet above the water that hold historic light houses but contain almost no surface tributaries flowing towards the Lake. Yet these Lakes hold 20% of all the surface fresh water on the entire planet and 500,000 gallons of water flows from Lake Superior into Lake Huron every second.[18] The surface area of the five Lakes is a combined 94,000 square miles.

The region is so large that although I would be inside it long enough to see only three of the five, it would take me two weeks to wind through the domain of the Great Lakes Watershed. I stayed over in Duluth for two nights and then I crossed the bridge over the St Louis River Delta feeding Lake Superior, also known as "Gichi-gami" or "great sea" by the Ojibwa, and into Wisconsin on the last day of July. I cut right through the heart of the Great Lakes region on the large peninsula jutting east that hangs off of the mainland of Wisconsin and known as the "UP," short for the Upper Peninsula. Even though it lies within the political boundaries of Michigan, its only connection to mainland Michigan, the Lower Peninsula, is over a 5 mile long, four-lane wide man-made bridge. And although the Great Lakes region covers such an enormous area, in the UP I could bump from the shore of Lake Superior to the shore of Lake Michigan easily in a single day.

Thirty-seven days and 1,707 miles after getting the hand written note from Biff in Glacier National Park, I finally reached Traverse City, Michigan. Two days before arriving in Traverse City I had camped along the south shoreline of the UP near the beaches of Lake Michigan at Hog Island State Forest Campground. And the day before that I had camped along the *north* shoreline of the UP overlooking Lake *Superior* at Bay Furnace Campground inside the city limits of Christmas, Michigan. The town of Christmas, population 400, owed its existence to the fact that they once had a huge stone blast furnace where ships plying the Great Lakes and carrying iron ore from the mines near Ely would stop and convert their raw loads into pig iron, an intermediary, mostly unusable iron product but lighter to ship.

Riding between the two Great Lake campgrounds I traversed the breadth of the UP during an 84 mile day. On the crossover from Lake Superior to Lake

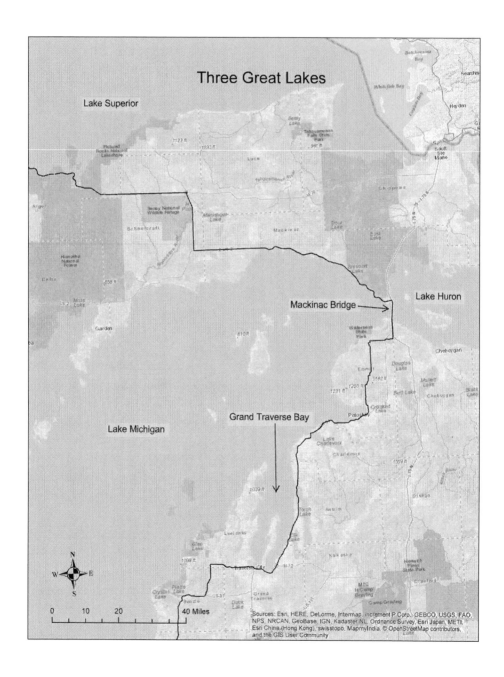

Michigan I had stopped for lunch in Blaney Park, a tiny town with 3 antique shops, about a dozen houses, a bed and breakfast, and surrounded by White Spruce trees. The rear wheel was starting to stress from the weight of my gear on the back rack and I had spent most of the day riding with one broken spoke in it. The front tire doesn't wear quite as fast as the rear one either and so during the last hour of sunlight on that crossover day in the campground along the wooded shoreline of Lake Michigan I rotated the tires while the rear wheel was off to replace the broken spoke.

The next day I made the big turn south and left US Highway 2 for good at the Mackinac Bridge. Out in the distance, I noticed the nearly 5 mile long suspension bridge, known as Big Mac, at least 45 minutes before actually arriving at the Straights of Mackinac19 because I had a clear view out over the broad open expanse of Lake Michigan while riding due East. The bridge itself ran perpendicular to my path of travel, and just to the right of my line of site, as it connects the two peninsulas of Michigan. The peninsulas had been connected by ferries until the bridge was opened in 1957. Although its main span between the two towers is 400 feet shorter than the Golden Gate, its total length is nearly 3 times longer. When I reached the bridge, a busy four-lane thoroughfare carrying I-75 traffic, the Michigan Department of Transportation would not let me cross it on bicycle. Not that I would want to. In fact, The Mackinac Bridge Authority has a "Drivers Assistance Program" available 24/7 that even provides drivers for motorists who are uncomfortable with driving across the Mackinac Bridge. I paid them one dollar to put my bicycle in a DOT pick-up truck and carry me across.

In Traverse City, just as I had in Culbertson, Montana, I stopped at a pay phone booth. Except this time, the price of a phone call having more than doubled, I put in a quarter before dialing the number. It seemed awkward and I didn't know what to expect. But Hanz had been expecting my call and almost immediately gave me directions to his house as though, like Biff, he had known me my whole life. He lived at the bottom of Lake Michigan's Grand Traverse Bay along a flat semi-circular shaped road that hugged the shoreline. A large pre-historic ice sheet was the architect of this geological design that created the slight spread to the 30-mile long "pinkie" finger of the "hand" of Michigan's Lower Peninsula. The ice sheet has come and gone many times and it actually sat on top of the pinkie just the same but the bedrock there was much harder than the surrounding earth and the ice couldn't quite grind it down enough to make it disappear beneath the waves when it last retreated. The bay is quite impressive and, as you stare out across the water, it seems as though you are looking at one of those seas described in the Old Testament. When I arrived, the wind was blowing in from the north under a sunny sky and small white caps were lapping up to the shore. Houses had been built on the opposite side of the road away from the shore, thereby leaving the bayside of the road looking like a preserved lagoon. It was a public space with such clear water that you could see the sandy bottom of Lake Michigan. Although no houses had been permitted to be built along the water, the homeowners were given a permanent easement, if they wanted, to build a dock in the shallow water of the bay yet anyone could swim there. It was a fantastic public-private partnership.

When I walked into Hanz's house, he immediately showed me where the shower was, took my dirty clothes, and put them into the washing machine. After cleaning up, he drove me over to an orchard to pick apples. "Sorry, but you are too late for the cherries," he said. Traverse City is sometimes called the Cherry Capital of the World. Five counties surrounding the bay and covering an area of 2,981 square miles with a population of 170,000 make up 40% of the tart cherry production in the United States.[20] Like Lake Superior, Lake Michigan is a large enough body of water to moderate the local climate. It soaks up heat in the summer to keep the cherry trees cool and protects them from intense cold in the winter. This climate, along with sandy, well-drained soils, makes it a primo area for growing cherries. It is the major driver of the economy and dominates the culture of the region.

Very near downtown Traverse City, at the bottom of this bowl-shaped shoreline that forms the southern boundary of Grand Traverse Bay, a narrow 15 mile-long, 1-1/2-mile wide peninsula juts upward into this vast bay from the mainland. It too was a bit too hard for the ice sheet to grind down. This mini-peninsula creates what seems like a long pier dividing Grand Transverse Bay into almost identical eastern and western halves from about mid "pinkie" on down. Island View Orchards is a fourth generation cherry farm on this peninsula that has been in continuous operation since 1876. A Swedish immigrant, the founder of Island View Orchards, purchased 40 acres of land on what was a wooded peninsula that today is surrounded by nature preserves, lighthouses, breweries, vacations spots, and wineries. It's a perfect haven for cherry production. But he didn't know it at the time. He didn't understand the advantageous ecological conditions of having land on a peninsula whose climate was perfectly moderated by one of the largest fresh bodies of water on the planet. He planted apples and potatoes. Not that apples didn't fare well and still do today. But cherries, oh boy! They would love the cool summers that Grand Traverse Bay was able to provide while also preventing crippling harsh winters experienced by the deep interior of mainland Michigan.

Finally, in 1925, about the same year my house in College Park was built, they planted Montmorency cherries, the tart variety that was in high demand to make the perfect cherry pie. Today, the farm is owned by a third generation grandson and his wife. His two brothers help with the daily operations, and, the next generation of sons, daughters, nieces, and nephews, along with 5 or 6 local kids, is temporarily employed during the July cherry harvest season. There is a migrant Mexican family group that is shared with other farms to help with the fall apple harvest. The farm has grown to 180 acres, a third of which is leased land. Seventy-five percent of the farm operation is in the Montmorency cherry. Over the years, the farm has also added the Balanton cherry, another sour variety that is much darker and that is used in cough syrup.[21]

More recently, the area has discovered that grapes do really well in the moderating climate around Lake Michigan as well. Island View Orchards has added 4 varieties of grapes that now make up 5% of the farm operations. In fact, the invasion of grapes into the Cherry Capital has sprung up a whole new commerce and tourism industry in Traverse City. Left Foot Charlie is an urban winery and cider maker in downtown that buys the grapes (and apples) from Island View Orchards. They stimulate local tourism with their tastings and tours, and then also ship product to bars and restaurants as far away as Chicago and New York City.

Hanz made his living as a stone mason. But he was diagnosed with multiple sclerosis the previous year - about the same time that he lost his mother to a car accident, his father to sickness, and his dog to epilepsy. His attitude was unbelievably positive. He knew that if he exercised, he could prevent the progression of the disease. He was 45 years old and as lean and fit as I was from having pedaled across seven states already. His new dog, a chocolate lab named Duchess, ran in front of the truck as we drove through the orchard. When we got back to Hanz's house, we had to take her down to the waterfront so that she could fetch sticks out of Lake Michigan. Hanz's boat was anchored off in the distance about 200 feet from the shoreline. The sun's light filtered through the clouds and a stiff summer breeze blew into our faces and pushed our hair back in wavy patterns as we stood on the clear sandy bottom of Traverse Bay. We could have been in one of those shampoo commercials. The wind created the choppy waves that splashed across Duchess' chest while we waited on her to bring our stick back. Although Duchess was swimming, it seemed as though the bay was shallow enough that we would have been able to walk all the way to the boat. It was a peaceful, meditative, almost prayerful scene. The sun was starting to set and so we went back to the house where Hanz's wife had supper ready for us to eat. She had made pork chops, fresh sweet corn, potatoes cooked in onions, a cucumber salad, and, of course, a fresh cherry pie.

IF IT WEREN'T FOR the large bodies of water, such as the inland freshwater seas known as the Great Lakes, and the oceans of the earth absorbing the heat, the effects of a warming climate would be much more dramatic in terms of what we "feel".[22] You might think of these enormous bodies of water as the "central HVAC units" of the planet. When we get these big snow falls you might say, "What global warming?" In 2017, the Rocky Mountains got more snow in January than they normally do all year.[23] The same huge snow event of 2017 in the Rockies, though, happened to be in the form of rain and flooding in the valleys of California. So much so that it brought California's Central Valley out of a drought that had been so severe that no one in this generation had ever experienced it and there is ecological and statistical evidence that this magnitude of drought had not been experienced by the last two generations either.[24] The ocean temperatures do not fluctuate from season to season like the air temperature does; they may fall a few degrees but the temperature baseline has been shifted upwards a bit. So when the oceans release some of their surface moisture, and if it happens to be winter, it falls as snow in the northern latitudes and in the higher elevations.

The heavy rains that occurred in the spring of 2017 just west of the Mississippi River received almost no media attention but they produced record breaking flows at fourteen US Geological Survey monitoring stations on several tributaries to the Mississippi River. At four of these, the previous record had been set only 16 months earlier.[25] The monitoring stations that broke the all-time record during the first week of May 2017 **and** 16 months previously (in parenthesis) were:

Illinois River near Watts, Oklahoma (Dec 28, 2015)
Gasconade River at Jerome, Missouri (Dec 30, 2015)
Gasconade River near Rich Fountain, Missouri (Dec 30, 2015)
Meramec River near Eureka, Missouri (Dec 30, 2015)

This would be the "flashing red light." Since these are all-time records, we can assume they are at least 100-year floods and quite possibly 500-year floods. Statistically speaking, the chance of a 500-year flood occurring in any one year is 0.2 percent (one-fifth of one percent or 2 out of a thousand). The chance of flipping a coin and getting heads twice in a row is 25% (0.5 X 0.5). The chance of having a 500-year flood two years in a row (technically, this is in 3 different calendar years but within 24 months of each other) might be

0.04% (4 out of ten thousand) - it's an unusual event. These are back-of- the-envelope statistics because we haven't taken into consideration all the other events happening around the globe. But we can deduce that the chances of these recent events happening is probably somewhere between these two ranges (0.2 and 0.04 percent). The oceans are storing most of the excess heat within the biosphere and then releasing huge volumes of surface evaporation due to the lowered activation energy or "threshold" energy; the temperature distance between the surface of the ocean and the temperature at which water molecules will turn into vapor or gas has narrowed. It's as though the water molecules have gotten easier to be plucked away into the clouds. They are like a ripe cherry or apple that is about to fall from the tree as compared to a sour one. In North America, these clouds of moisture start off the coast of the Pacific Ocean, generally blow east, and then dump their moisture when they hit a cold front. Voila! – Record floods two years in a row. The rural community of Pocahontas, Arkansas, was probably hit the hardest with satellite data estimating the flooding to be six miles wide!

But if you want a true barometer of climate conditions, take a look at the glaciers in the world. Glaciers do not grow and recede on the whims of daily weather patterns. They are the slow and steady ice machines. If the global climate is warming they slowly recede and if it is cooling, they slowly advance; regardless of what individual drought or rain or snow events that are happening locally, the pace of the glaciers remain consistent. It is really no different than how a stock portfolio works on Wall Street. If you are in a bull market and equities are rising at a clip of say, 8% a year, at the end of the year your portfolio will be worth 8% more. However, there may be days you lose a thousand dollars and there are other days that you gain more than 8% of the portfolio's worth. It's all what they call "noise" because when it's all said and done at the end of the year, if you had a portfolio that was worth $100,000 at the beginning of the year, it's going to be worth $108,000 on December 31 no matter what the daily fluctuations were throughout the year. And vice versa; no matter what the ups and downs were through the year, in a bear market, your portfolio is going to be worth less. Likewise, the glaciers tell no lies. They don't care what the daily fluctuations are in your neighborhood. The simply reflect the overall trend that is occurring. In Glacier National Park, the glaciers are mere remnants of what they were when my maternal grandfather immigrated to America from Slovenia during World War I. In fact, I saw not one glacier, not even a small glimpse, on the climb up to Logan Pass. They have receded too high into the upper elevations in one generation that none are visible without a hike up into the alpine backcountry.

In the summer of 2004, I met up with my parents in Calgary, Alberta, and we drove to the Columbia Icefields in Banff and Jasper National Parks along the Continental Divide that extends northward above Glacier National Park. The Columbia Icefield can best be described as a flat, plateau like area that holds year-round ice and feeds six major glaciers. The ice has formed from centuries of accumulated snow compacting on itself. It is the freezer of the Rockies. The Icefield is basically a frozen lake that has outlets in several different directions atop of a major watershed divide; except the outlets are slow flowing glaciers instead of fast flowing streams; whether melting or growing, glaciers do move by gravity, but just much slower than liquid water. The depth of the ice in many places would bury the Eiffel Tower and it covers 125 square miles. But that number is changing as we speak. Within the icefield there are mountain peaks that poke up kind of like the way candles rise above the white icing on a birthday cake. When you are driving along the Icefields Parkway in the seam between mountain ridges, you cannot see the Icefield itself; you would need to be in a helicopter and look down upon it. But you can catch glimpses of the toes of glaciers poking out. One of these glaciers, the Athabasca Glacier, nearly reaches the Icefields Parkway, the toe of which is within walking distance from the Icefield Information Centre. You can park there and actually walk on top of it. In 1870, the Athabasca Glacier's toe would have poked into the Icefield Information Centre's lobby and parking lot. Today it is a 1 mile walk to it. The walk gets farther every year.

Another interesting feature in Banff National Park is the Crow Foot Glacier. It was named by early French fur trade explorers because from the seam above where the Icefields Parkway now runs, there were three toes that were visible where the glacier spilled down between small ridges and resembled the spread out claws of a bird. At one time it was fed from above by a smaller plateau-like area, separated from the Columbia Icefield but nearby, called the Wapta Icefield. Today the glacier is isolated and completely cut off from the shrinking Wapta Icefield. And one of the "claws" has receded away from view and it no longer resembles the image for which it was named.

WHEN I LEFT TRAVERSE City, Michigan, the character of the trip changed. I felt lonely and isolated. I couldn't figure out a way to get anywhere without zig zagging on county roads that didn't head directly south. It was a complete maze of roads and my head was spinning - Silver Lake Road, then the M-22, then right, left, right, left around pocket lakes, and diversions on cut-throughs around the mirage of nooks and crannies that is the shoreline of Lake

Michigan. This not only created navigation frustration but it meant that I had no hope of coming across another riding companion as it would be impossible to funnel and concentrate the few cross-country cyclist out there on a major corridor. Who else is crisscrossing northwest mainland Michigan by bicycle and would they even be on the same roads that I was choosing? Finally I found a freeway at Ludington, Michigan and a policeman soon pulled me over.

After looking over my driver's license, he said, "Son, I don't know what you people do in Alabama but here in Michigan a bicycler...Cannot...Be...on the Freeway!"

"Can I go down to the next exit and get off?" I asked.

"No sir. There is an overpass right there," he said pointing at a hill leading up to a bridge over the freeway. "You need to leave now."

"Yes sir"

I removed the panniers from the bicycle and carried them up the hill to the bridge overpass above the freeway. Then I walked back down and strained to push my bicycle through tall grass and around scraggly, unmaintained shrubs and saplings up to the road.

The cop watched me, as though I might disobey his orders. From up above and looking down at him, I watched him nod approvingly. He got in his car and drove off.

Regardless, the cop had every right to kick me off the freeway because it is what Michigan law says. But it was like I didn't belong there just in general and it gave me pause for a second. Now my head was swirling with emotions. I was angry and sad at the same time. I wanted to be home. I was sorely disappointed and shocked that I couldn't ride on a nice wide shoulder again. The irony was the fact that I was actually safer on the freeway with the 5-foot wide shoulder than I was with cars whizzing past my outside pedal and left elbow on a two lane county road with no shoulder. On my very first day way back in Washington, in the urbanized area around Everett, US 2 had been a limited access divided freeway, much like the one I had just been kicked off, but state law there did not prohibit me from being there.

Looking back now on this incident also reminds me of what rights we do have to prevent police from overstepping their authority. The fourth amendment to the Constitution is beautifully and elegantly written in fifty-four words. Forgive me for indulging but here is a reminder of what the fourth amendment is: It says that if a policeman or policewoman knocks on my door and says that they would like to take a look inside, I can say, "Please get off of my property," because the fourth amendment makes it clear that "The right of the people to be secure in their persons, houses, papers, and effects, against unreasonable searches and seizures, shall not be violated..." He or she is, however, allowed to search my house "upon probable cause" if there is suspect of a crime committed. But not before he has obtained a signed warrant from a judge whereby the warrant was "supported by oath or affirmation, and particularly describing the place to be searched, and the persons or things to be seized."

Two days later I crossed into my eighth state, Indiana, where the roads ran in a more familiar, more direct, grid-like pattern through farmland. I was determined to cross three more state lines.

Hanz and Duchess looking out over Grand Traverse Bay

Below the Divide

"Remember Red, hope is a good thing, maybe the best of things, and no good thing ever dies." - Andy Dufresne, *The Shawshank Redemption*

I ARRIVED IN COLUMBUS, Indiana, on August 17. But before I reached Columbus, Indiana,I had had several people offer me room and board. I took a few of them up on the offer. I was running low on funds and the companionship was refreshing. The ride became lonelier after I had turned south. When I was paralleling the Canadian border, I saw riders in both directions every day. But now other riders were far and few between. Along the Hi-Line, people riding bicycles were on a mission, going long distances to get somewhere. And the road was straight and wide with a clean shoulder. After I had turned south at the Straits of Mackinac, they were as likely to be homeless and wandering without purpose. I was as likely to get a "rebel" yell and a beer can thrown at me as I was to get a thumbs-up. It was a mix of despondency on my part, contempt on the part of drivers, and good-hearted hospitality from the local communities along the way.

One night in a public campground near Albion, Indiana, I was camping near a group of Mormons. They came in while I was cooking supper. I had just set up my tent and had not yet paid for my spot when the ranger came by and asked if I were with their group. The lady in charge jumped in and emphatically said, "Yes. He is with us."

I became sick at one point and had no energy to pedal for three days. A man named Joginder, who came to the US from Uganda, Africa, when the narcissistic Idi Amin took over his country, took me in and fed me three meals a day until I could continue my trip. His compassion almost makes me cry as I write this. I was ready to give up and this total stranger from a continent thousands of miles away and a place I have only read about in news stories gave me what I really needed most – hope.

I had pulled into Marquette, Michigan, looking for a place to rest for a few days and maybe go see a doctor. I asked someone if there happened to be a hostel in town. They said, "No, but North Michigan University is out of session and they rent dorm rooms for seventeen dollars a night during the summer."

I don't remember how I met Joginder but he was there coaching at a boxing camp for Olympic hopefuls. He came to my door and knocked on it 3 times a day to make sure I was eating. He took me to the cafeteria and absolutely refused to let me pay for my own meals.

Back in Montana, people in the isolated prairie towns had been happy to see us and had pointed us to the city park to set up our tents and get hot water from the bathroom; many even had showers installed in the bathrooms. One day in North Dakota, bikers heading west asked me to deliver a postcard to a friend they knew at The Base in Ely. At Bay Furnace Campground in the UP, a couple from Stockton, California, had made me breakfast before I left. At Hog

Island Campground, another couple had offered me supper while I was fixing the spoke in the rear wheel. South of the Mackinac Bridge, it seemed as though people were a tad more leery of strangers. One night in a rural area of Indiana, a state park ranger on midnight patrol shone a flashlight through the tent mesh and told me that I was camping in an illegal spot. Even though he was kind enough to let me go freely, without recourse, and even helped move me to a group camping spot, it was disconcerting to be awoken and put in a groggy confusion.

On the way to the proper camping area, we met a man named Berman, who I will always remember by his firm handshake. He was from the local area but was camping at the park with a church retreat. He knew the park ranger and struck up a conversation with him while I stood waiting.

Finally Berman looked at me and said, "Why don't you just stay under the awning of my camper instead of trying to re-set your tent."

The ranger looked at me and nodded his head in agreement. The next morning Berman gave me coffee and breakfast and asked me if I needed money before I left.

In Columbus, Indiana, I met a kind, gracious, family man named Emanuele at the local Catholic Church. He took me to his house so that I could get a shower and then took me out to dinner. Emanuele was an Italian born in Holland, and raised both in the Netherlands and in Indianapolis. We talked about all sorts of topics including the meaning of success, how to raise children, the ideals of American society. We met some of his friends at the café and he would often use the word "amigo" in reference to the person to whom he was speaking. For him though, our relationship would be transient and there would be no sentimental good byes. It was just two people crossing paths serendipitously, nothing more. No thought of sending a Christmas card or anything too committal like that. He was simply doing his duty to help a visitor in his own hometown. Although we could go into deep discussions about our personal lives, the relationship would end forever the moment I pedaled away.

I left the Great Lakes Watershed by crossing over the St. Lawrence River Divide somewhere along State Road 9 in northern Indiana a few days before. I had left the shore of Lake Michigan a few days before that. I had crossed the Divide at 955 feet elevation. From the shore of Lake Michigan to where the St. Lawrence Divide crosses Indiana State Road 9, it is 125 miles as the crow flies. I had been gaining about 3 feet in elevation for every mile I pedaled but I never noticed. From the time I crossed the divide in northern Indiana to Columbus, I had thus been on a downhill ride at about the same pace in reverse but I never noticed it either; neither the climb nor the descent appreciably affected how fast I rode, how many miles I traveled in a day, or how hungry I was.

THE ICE SHEET THAT sat on top of North America during the height of the last ice age probably extended all the way down to about where Columbus, Indiana, sits today. It definitely would have covered all of the present day Great Lakes and most certainly would have extended down to at least the St. Lawrence Divide I had crossed in the northern part of the state. It most likely poked its nose, the very terminal part that poured out melt water, somewhere between the Divide and where the Ohio River Valley sits today. The sheet of ice would have been hundreds or even thousands of feet thick, plowed down everything in its path, and gouged the earth as it advanced, the weight of it being unimaginable. The ice, being in a continuous slow movement even once it reached its furthest extent, would have stopped growing because of warmer temperatures in the southern latitudes melting the nose away. Imagine feeding an endless Popsicle to a child who keeps licking the end so that the length of the stick of ice never changes.

When the climate warmed and the ice sheet retreated, rudimentary rivers were formed on the top of the granite bedrock crust of the earth to carry away the meltwater that came in increasing amounts. This crust of the earth is many miles thick and where the Great Lakes sit today, the crust of the earth was made of a much softer sedimentary rock. So when the ice sheet retreated to where it now sits at the North Pole, deep and massive pockets had been gouged out that immediately filled with the fresh meltwater from the Wisconsinan Glacier, the part of the ice sheet that existed in what we know today as the Great Lakes region. It took a hundred thousand years for the ice sheet to reach its maximum extent. The time chart that scientists have created that depicts the growth of this ice sheet looks similar to a trending stock on the Dow Jones Industrial Average. Over time it goes up a little and down a little but the upward gains outpace the downward losses and looking from a distance, over a long period, the stock has a definite overall trend; eventually it reaches a plateau and no longer grows in value and then begins to decline. Although the ice sheet similarly slowly grew - 2 steps forward, 1 step back, and so forth - for tens of thousands years, it only took about 10 centuries for the ice to retreat far enough back to reveal the Great Lakes.[26]

IT WOULD BE AMISS to call Columbus, Indiana the architectural capital of the world. It would be too pretentious for such a "young" town to try to compete with the iconic European cities or even other ancient cities on other continents. But it might be able to be called the architectural inspiration of the world. As one visitor put it, "Even the bus stops are cool." How this nondescript prairie town, squeezed between the White River and its tiny tributary called Haw Creek, reached worldwide notoriety can be attributed to the vision of Joseph Irwin Miller, the man who had to figure out a way to attract highly skilled employees for his new company, the Cummins Engine Company, during the post-World War II boom. So he established the Cummins Foundation to subsidize architectural design a little more snazzy than the run-of-the-mill school buildings stoic Midwesterners might try to build. Before long, other types of projects began to get special funding too and today Columbus is known as the "Athens of the Prairie.[27]"

The next day, I crossed the Ohio River and into Louisville, Kentucky. To be honest with myself, I was tired of riding. Even the rural state routes through the UP had adequate shoulders but the roads here had almost none and it was mentally exhausting keeping up with what traffic was behind me and constantly glancing over my shoulder. It was more like a sideways glance with my eyes, while trying *not* to move my head too much, and getting as much information as possible from my peripheral vision. Your peripheral vision is always working but most of the time you are not conscious of it. So there was this continuous conscious effort to keep my peripheral vision "turned on." It took a lot of effort and I could almost feel the extra calories being burned by my brain.

I reached my home state on August 25. I did 285 miles in the last 3 days. It was so hot and humid that I had salt residues piled on my skin after each day. Bent over with my head buried in my shirt and my arms flailing in front of me, I peeled my shirt off before going to bed. After leaving Louisville, I spent one night at Beaver Creek Campground on Barren River Lake just outside Glasgow, Kentucky. I spent one night in Tennessee at Cedars of Lebanon State Park, about half way across the state, and then crossed the Alabama state line the next day. Physically I could have gone on forever but I was mentally drained. The narrow roads had pushed me to my limits, especially trying to navigate them on a loaded down bicycle that was slow to turn and slow to stop as though I were steering a battleship. I had been breaking a spoke in the rear wheel once a day now. I had extras taped to the frame and had been replacing them every evening at camp. My Dad drove up from Birmingham and picked me up. I was out-of-gas and my trip was over.

I had been over two mountain ranges, through 3 time zones, through 4 continental watersheds, and had ridden three thousand two hundred and twenty-one miles. In an automobile, I could have easily completed this distance in less than a week; in a plane it would have taken a few hours. But I had used only 6 percent of the energy requirements of an efficient passenger car.[28] That is like saying that although my house is worth $250,000, I just bought it for fifteen thousand dollars; on an energy scale, the bicycle is an incredible bargain. It is the perfect balance between time and energy. If I had walked the distance I had just traveled I would have expended not 6% of the energy of a passenger car but 10%, and it would have taken over half a year to do it. I had done it in 57 days.

MY MOTHER CALLED TO say that dad wasn't doing well...that I really needed to get over to the hospital. So I left work early and walked to the bus stop to catch the local 10 to the train station. I got off the train at Lindberg and hopped the number 6 to Emory Hospital. On the way, I got a text from my aunt that dad had been moved down to the fifth floor to hospice care. I was feeling a lot of anxiety. It didn't help that the bus driver was new to the route and was reading directions from a piece of paper while driving. I had been on the route once or twice before but couldn't remember if we were exactly on the right road. I would catch a familiar site out of the window and say to myself, "We're good." As we were approaching the left hand turn lane onto Clifton Road, the bus driver was staying in the right lane. My anxiety grew and grew until at the last possible moment someone on the bus yelled, "Left!" The driver looked in his mirror and swerved left. He then asked, "Is everybody all right!!?"

Dad did make it through that day, and every day after work I made the same journey over to the hospital. The next day I was again seated on the number 6 behind the bus driver and I picked up a small bit of conversation she had with a patron getting on at a bus stop in mid route. From her answers I sensed that the bus driver was new to the route. I moved over to the right side of the bus so that I could look straight out the windshield. As she approached the left turn lane onto Clifton Road she was staying in the right lane a bit too long.

Finally, I said, "You need to take a left."

She said, "What?"

"You need to take a left."

"Here?"

"Yes!" I shouted.

She looked in her mirror, swerved left, cut off a car entering the turn lane, and stopped in the middle of the intersection. When it was clear that no one would be hit, she continued on.

Vehicular traffic in the US creates sixteen times more emissions than every single bus running across the entire country. Vehicular traffic in the US creates **200** times the amount of emission than all the jet airplanes taking off from the airport one mile south of my backyard, the busiest in the world - 1000 daily take-offs and two planes landing at the same time on parallel runways every 90 seconds for 12 hours straight.[29] Let me say that another way; the sheer volume of us riding on top of our personal tailpipes overwhelms jet airplanes and big buses combined. Even airplanes are a form of public transportation when you compare them to the inefficiency of moving a person around in a box on four wheels. If I don't get out and walk, ride, or use a bus, who is? I don't have to ride a bicycle 500 miles the next time I go visit my distant relatives but I *have* stopped looking for a parking spot right by the front door.

IT MIGHT HAVE BEEN surprising enough that the Clayton County Commissioner Chambers was standing room only. But what was really surprising was the fact that it was standing room only on a Saturday morning... on the day after the 4th of July Holiday. The topic of discussion was whether or not to allow the citizens of Clayton County to vote on whether or not the county would join the Metropolitan Atlanta Rapid Transit Authority as a full-fledged member. Let me repeat the topic of discussion on that July 5th holiday weekend that needed to be decided in an emergency meeting: it was *not* to *join* MARTA. It was to simply *allow* a referendum on the issue in the upcoming November general elections.

There were 4 commissioners at the bench that day and Jay Tifton, the Chair, had been leading the charge ever since the state legislature passed the bill to allow local municipalities to raise their sales tax one penny if they used it to fund public transportation. The glitch was that the referendum had to be during a general gubernatorial election season and this was a general election year. And the other glitch was that the ability to raise sales tax expired after this year. So it was now or never. One commissioner was absent – probably had scheduled holiday plans in advance – but her constituents were there in large numbers and must have taken notice.

There had been three public hearings on the issue since March. And those discussions seemed to have been dominated by one commissioner there that day named Mitch Eagleton. He wanted, at most, one-half penny sales tax to be used for MARTA. In exchange there would be no hope for any fixed transit such as rail. He even pulled me to the side in the parking lot one day after a public hearing and whispered, "There will be a snowball's chance in hell the day Clayton County joins MARTA for a whole penny."

In the beginning he got his way; the commissioners had approved the referendum for a one-half penny sales tax at the June regular meeting. The MARTA board had immediately convened an emergency meeting the day after and said, "No. Even if the referendum passes we won't accept Clayton County as a member for one-half penny. You would be tying into a system that the other members, Fulton and DeKalb counties, have been contributing with one-penny sales tax revenue for the past 40 years to build and operate a robust system with 110 bus routes, 48 miles of rail, and 38 stations." The haggling still continued on that Saturday with everything in the balance. Whether or not to place the issue on the November referendum had to be done within 120 days of the general election and so it was that day or never. Eagleton would not budge and one other commissioner was firmly with Chairman Tifton; it was essentially deadlocked 2-2.

At the "eleventh hour," just before the meeting was to adjourn and after a lot of haggling, one commissioner changed her mind and declared, "I'll vote yes" and swung the vote 3-1. The room burst into a roar and chaos; grown men and women were crying. The referendum passed that November by a crushing 78-22 margin of victory. Needless to say, the one commissioner who was not there lost her seat two years later and Mitch Eagleton lost his 2 years after that. And I could now catch the bus to Forest Park for the first time without worrying whether or not I had some extra change in my pocket.

TWENTY-SIX YEARS AFTER crossing the Alabama line on my bicycle, I was firmly rooted in my suburban community of College Park, Georgia. But are we really suburban? By the standards of population density, we certainly are. However, being next to the busiest airport in the world, there is a lot of land below the flight paths that has no residents and that fact skews the true density. By the standard of distance from the center of the urban core (7 miles) of the ninth largest metro area in the U.S., we *could* be, and when the town was incorporated in 1891, it certainly was. On the other hand, the urban core is only 5 metro stops away and the community has no less than 6 metropolitan transit buses zigzagging through the community; if you were to sit through a funeral service at the Episcopal Church on East Main Street, you might notice a slight vibration in your seat every four and a half minutes as the metro train rumbled by at 60 miles an hour and think "I must be in the city." But if I were to drop you inside the Ward 4 where there are brick ranches on half acre lots, you would say, "No, this is the suburbs." If I dropped you off in the residential areas around the old depot where early 20th century bungalows sit on 50-foot wide lots near 4-story upscale apartments, you would say, "No, this is urbane." If you saw the Family Dollar store sitting on top of an expansive parking lot along Virginia Avenue, you might be inclined to lean towards suburbia. After you walked from that parking lot and down the sidewalk six blocks to a café on Main Street, "Nope, it's the city."

Regardless, I had lived here long enough to gain enough institutional knowledge of the place that I could quote figures out of the 112 million dollar annual city budget. I knew the balance on every one of the thirteen revenue bonds our city owed. I knew the city manager on a first name basis and most of the city's department heads. I also knew the homeless people by name that lived along the railroad line. About this time, I got caught up in a battle with the governing body of the city over an issue whereby they wanted to sell another 36 million dollar bond, making it the 14th one, and pay $9 million out of reserves as a down payment to build a professional sports arena for the minor league team affiliated with the Atlanta Hawks. I hired an attorney because the notice for the court proceedings to validate the bond sale said in part "Any citizen...in the City of College Park...who has a right to object may intervene and become a party to these proceedings."

And so we did. On the appointed day of the proceedings in Fulton County Superior Court with the honorable Deputy Chief John J. Groger presiding, our plan was to object on the grounds that a municipality can't go into debt for recreational facilities that the community doesn't use. We had 7 citizens and the councilman from Ward 4, the sole "no" vote on the bond resolution, to show up. When I sat down in the courtroom, Councilman George said, "John, there is $150,000 worth of attorneys in here representing the city!"

It was hard to tell who was who but as I looked around the courtroom, there seemed to be about six attorneys to help represent the city. The city must have been a bit worried. Then about 5 minutes before the start of the hearing, one of them walked over to my attorney and handed him a surety bond for 5 million dollars. A surety bond was designed under Georgia statute to prevent a person from filing a frivolous lawsuit. Georgia law says that if a person files a suit against someone, the defendant has a right to claim attorney fees and other damages such as lost time and wages from having to defend themselves if they win. The surety bond was a way to hold the plaintiff accountable and let him know that he would be liable if he lost the case and it let him know that fact *before* the proceedings began. The problem is that I wasn't filing a lawsuit. I was simply becoming "a party to the proceedings." They were the ones who had filed for the validation. They were so scared of me and my one attorney that they had come up with a plan to circumvent basic democratic principles at the local level. It would have been akin to suppressing someone's right to free speech. To me it felt akin to a book burning. Even more than that, I knew these people – the mayor, all the councilman, all the department heads and had known them for years. You can't hold a public hearing? If you have the city's best interest at heart shouldn't you be able to defend a 36 million dollar publicly held bond? The judge let the proceedings go forth and I was called to the witness stand.

"Mr. Duke, here are your Facebook posts. Aren't you really on a political campaign to smear the mayor?" asked one of the attorneys representing the city.

"Madam, I am fighting this bad deal on two fronts – it is both a financial and political battle. They cannot be separated"

She then asked me, "Mr. Duke, how much did you pay your attorney?"

I looked past the city attorney standing in front of me and directly at my attorney sitting at the table and then at the judge and then back at my attorney looking for guidance. My attorney nodded at me in affirmation but it still seemed to me to be an irrelevant question so I turned back to the judge and asked, "Do I have to answer that?"

The judge reprimanded me by saying, "You are to answer questions not ask them."

"Fifteen hundred dollars," I replied.

In the end the judge ruled in my favor on a technicality and so the surety bond became a moot point. But he did allow the validation of the bond once the technicality had been fixed.

Even though we didn't stop our city from going over the 200 million dollar mark in total indebtedness over a development that had been tailored for a bunch of guys in Ralph Lauren three-piece suits who lived God-knows-where and who looked at our community as a cash cow, we, and what I mean by "we" is those citizens who went to the courtroom and council meetings and who gave financial donations to support some of my legal fees, built quite a bit of political capital of our own. We put enough political pressure on the city to oust the one incumbent councilman who enthusiastically supported the bad deal. Here is how I worded my thoughts at a council meeting 14 months before filing the objection:

"I am sure you have heard of the Paris Accords on Climate Change. Mayors from many cities from around the world were there. While they were discussing solutions to this enormous challenge, there was another meeting next door called the Paris Accords To Build More Professional Sports Venues With Other People's Money. You might have been there.

"You don't even know what it is going to cost to build a venue for a wealthy basketball organization known as the Atlanta Hawks. Yet you have made a blind commitment. According to the City Manager, it would cost between ten and forty million dollars. That is like saying Wayfield has milk for sale for somewhere between a dollar and four dollars a gallon. I have seen this council agonize over whether or not to fund a part-time, twenty-five thousand dollar city staff position. But now you throw around these million dollar figures as though you might be Warren Buffet or Bill Gates. But you are not. It is our money. To build this arena, you will to have to: 1) Deplete city savings 2) Divert tax revenues that were being used somewhere else or 3) Sell bonds and be in debt"

All three happened in the end. The final tab on the project, which is being built as we speak, currently sits at 46 million. I then went on to summarize:

"But the arena project is about status and another way of 'keeping up with the Joneses.' It is a project that creates a boondoggle that we have to maintain forever. The Atlanta Hawks will contemptuously call us 'sucker' underneath their breath for funding their project. No other business entity gets this type of corporate welfare. If they want to have an arena in College Park, then let them buy the land and build it themselves as a private endeavor just like everybody else has to do."

I DON'T KNOW IF one can fully understand the importance of protecting the public domain for the general welfare of all, know the lives that other people live, and see the daunting environmental challenges that we impact in our everyday choices without getting out of your car, without riding a bus once in a while, without seeing how other communities do things, handle problems, and manage resources, without feeling the wind blow against your face, without following through on your convictions, quite frankly, without leaving the suburbs.

I do know that natural resources must be managed and public policy has to be hammered out. You can choose not to do anything and leave things in the status quo but that is a choice in itself that has consequences. Just different ones. Think of it like this: instead of choosing a policy you can choose a consequence. We could set policy tightly or loosely or not at all. There are real costs involved where real dollars get spent and real cash flows when we don't choose wisely – it could be cash flowing through the hands of an individual who is building wealth of their own on paper yet has no regard for the local community or it might flow through the public health infrastructure and social net whereby the costs get subtly and covertly spread out among all of us. Either way, there are ramifications for managing or not managing all these things that belong to us as a whole, whether that be roads and bridges, bike paths, water resources, public transportation, or anything that we depend on for a modern functioning society. You can't have everything. You can't build a professional sports arena without something else being sacrificed. In my own community, we spent millions to build the arena and there are cracked up sidewalks, prominent bus stops with no shelters, and debris on the streets that seems to sit too long. If I don't object to bond debt that doesn't fix these problems, who is?

As I write this, the amount of CO_2 in the atmosphere went over a new threshold. On top of the Mauna Loa volcano in Hawaii sits an observatory run by the US Geological Survey. They have been measuring atmospheric CO_2 levels there every month since March of 1958. On that very first reading atmospheric CO_2 was 315 parts per million (ppm). In March of 2015 it crossed the 400 mark.[30] When the Wisconsinan Glacier sat on top of the Great Lakes, atmospheric CO_2 hovered around 180 ppm and it took about seven thousand years for CO_2 to rise to the earth's most upper "baseline" level of about 300 parts per million while the ice sheet was pulling back to the North Pole.[31]

The earth breathes in and out so to speak on two scales – one yearly and one centa-millennially (every 100,000 years). On a yearly basis, the earth's atmospheric CO_2 reaches a peak in May and then begins to decline as spring foliage in the northern hemisphere reaches full bloom and plants are photosynthesizing at maximum efficiency. It seems that since the southern atmosphere, whose seasons are opposite those in the northern atmosphere, has lost its foliage by May that there would be no difference no matter when you measured atmospheric CO_2. However, the southern hemisphere is dominated by oceans and the sheer volume of plant biomass in the northern hemisphere as compared to the southern hemisphere drives the annual cycle of fluctuating CO_2.[32] The earth is "inhaling" from May to November and "exhaling" from November to May. But the total accumulation of atmospheric CO_2 has trended upward, like a credit card that never quite gets paid off and continues to accumulate charges.

The earth also breathes on a grand scale in which the inhale and exhale occurs over a period of about 1000 centuries. It's as though the yearly fluctuations are shallow breaths and then there is a big sigh every once in a while. The direct driver of this long cycle has to do with a slight wobble, the Milankovitch wobble, in the earth's rotation around the sun. The Milankovitch wobble is like a bicycle wheel that wavers from side to side because it is missing a spoke. It is this wobble that sets off a chain reaction of events that correlates with the slow fall in atmospheric CO2 over tens of millennia, down to about 180ppm as the earth cools, and then, as the earth wobbles back, seems to cause a relatively sudden rise (7000 years) back to what has consistently been a peak of about 300 parts per million. This pattern is repeated over and over. The rising CO2 may not be what *directly* caused the Wisconsinan Glacier to *begin* to back away from Columbus, Indiana, but it most likely amplified and accelerated its retreat back to the North Pole in the end.[33]

The question we should be asking ourselves is "Where is the current upward trend in atmospheric CO2 going to end?" We are adding a tiny fraction every day. Take a look at one of those debt clocks and see the numbers twirling. With CO2 we added 2.4 ppm in 2017 and about 23 ppm over the previous decade since 2017. The decade of the 1960's we added about 8 ppm, in the 1970's we added about 13 ppm, the 1980's it was about 16, the 1990's it was only about 15, and the 2000's it was about 19. The overall trend seems to be generally *accelerating* at about 3 ppm every decade and we will hit the 500 mark in the year 2058 if not sooner. What is that going to be like? If ppm's were currency and one ppm were a 100 dollar bill, the debt clock would be "spinning" at 65 cents a day. That may not sound like a lot but if the earth itself were measured in parts per million relative to our solar system, its mass would only be 3 ppm. To put it another way you could be charged with driving under the influence if the amount of alcohol in your bloodstream were 800 ppm.[34]

It is incredible to think that we do have the power to tweak the climate. It is like putting your foot on the scale behind your wife while she is trying to weigh herself. But what is also intriguing to me is the fact that, if indeed birth is a random event and every human life has the same value, the odds of me being born within a community of such extraordinary means that I can just take the time to peddle home from one side of the continent to the other is about 1 in 5.[35] The odds of me being born during such a small window of the great span of time whereby civilization is at peace and prospering enough for a person to freely and safely travel as I did, I would not even know how to begin to calculate. With that in mind how could I ever complain about anything? The heat and cold, the wind and rain that I experienced on my cross-continental journey, I could not have fathomed fretting about such things. To do so would have only aggravated any troubles that I might have encountered.[36]

It also would make me seem insensitive, unaware, and conceited. Because the fact of the matter is that the vast majority of the world lives on less than the equivalent of 10 US dollars a day.[37] They spend every waking moment just fulfilling the basic needs of life. Poverty in the US runs at about 13% and the poorest adults in the US, about twenty-four million, work and live on a minimum wage in which housing consumes most of their income.[38] If the other 4 out of 5 people in the world were to climb the social ladder to my middle class status, including those in my own country *and* in the developing world, the environmental impact would be the equivalent of increasing the world's population 12 times over.[39] They, the poor, are the ones who are riding the bus, walking, riding a bicycle as a fundamental form of transportation to really get somewhere and go about their day. They have the smallest environmental footprint of us all. If not for the poor among us, there would be even less of a public transportation network; asthma rates from ground level ozone would be even higher; the roads even more congested. And a rapidly warming climate would be more daunting than it already is. So why do we subconsciously and culturally view those standing at a bus stop in the rain or walking on a worn dirt path along the side of the road as second class citizens just because we haven't yet finished investing in basic infrastructure?

SIX MONTHS AFTER THE bond was approved to build the arena, I had re-built a decent enough relationship back to the mayor that he agreed to listen to some of my ideas. He would be up for re-election within the next 18 months when I sat down with him and asked for his support to finish The Brady Trail. The Brady Trail was a 10-foot wide multi-purpose bicycle and pedestrian pathway that had never been completed and had sat at a dead-end in the middle of a forested area next to the municipal golf course for over 10 years. The trail was to be finished along a tributary stream to the Chattahoochee River. I was to be paid for the environmental assessment, design, negotiating a corner easement from a residential property, and would basically manage the rest of the project nearly pro-bono. The funds for the project would come from sales tax revenues collected by the county and paid to the city solely for transportation projects. In late summer, the mayor sponsored the legislation and the council approved it unanimously.

Less than a year earlier I had stood in front of the them and had defiantly pointed my finger at each individual on the governing body and said "By God we will remind the citizens at the next election how you heavily subsidized a wealthy professional sports team." Soon after, city budget meetings started and I attended every one of them. At the very first one I had sat in the small cramped conference room no bigger than my kitchen for 2 hours and was ready to go home when the meeting was over. Then as everyone was collecting their things the mayor said,

"Before we go I've got one thing else I want you to discuss."

Councilman George said, "You can talk about it all you want. I am a "no" vote and I am going home." And he got up and walked out the door.

I stayed seated and the atmosphere got chaotic to say the least. The mayor wanted the council to vote on a 250,000 dollar tax break to an apartment building that had just been built next to the MARTA station. The mayor said matter-of-factly that, "It's about $250 dollars on each citizen of College Park."

The Ward 1 councilman was a meticulous engineer who read and analyzed every document word for word that ever came before the governing body. His ward included the most prominent homes on the premier residential street of Rugby Avenue where 200-year-old oaks line the street and included the historic building owned by the prestigious Woman's Club at the corner of Main Street. He had stayed seated and said, "You know my position on this. My answer is no." He argued that tax breaks are used as incentives to bring in development but this project was already built.

The Ward 3 councilman tried to convince the Ward 1 councilman that the developer of the apartment building, who was asking for help, is promising more high-end development near the MARTA station in the near future. So the Ward 1 councilman seemed to feel as though he was being brow beaten and in exasperation declared, "Mayor, it just doesn't feel right."

I asked if I could speak and the mayor immediately said, "No."

Meanwhile, the Ward 2 councilman, who had just ousted the incumbent over the arena deal and who had been a former city sanitation worker, was sitting quietly through his very first budget meeting. The mayor called for a break in the meeting and let the Ward 1 and Ward 3 councilmen go into the hallway and resolve their differences. While they were in the hall, I walked over to the stenographer and asked if the meeting was being recorded. The mayor jumped in and said, "Yes it's being recorded!"

I said, "Sir I was speaking to the stenographer."

"It's not your place to run the meeting but you are welcome to listen."

"There is no doubt about that."

"If you want to get cross-ways I will have you removed!"

"For what?"

"For runnin' yore mouth."

I chuckled and went back to my seat. When the two councilmen came back into the room from their hallway sidebar, the mayor called for a vote. The Ward 1 councilman had suddenly and miraculously changed his mind and the tax break was approved.

I did an open records request the very next day to obtain the 2-hour audio, clipped out the 20 minute piece about the tax break, and was ready to post it on the neighborhood Facebook page. But before I did that, I wanted the developer to give his side of the story. I really wanted the bike trail finished and had been at the meetings in the first place to see how I could get the funding. First I went to see the mayor privately and without an appointment to let him know that there was nothing personal between us and that it was just business. He thanked me and shook my hand.

When the developer and I sat down at the local bar-and-grill he knew something was up. We small talked for a few minutes and then he asked, "What is it that you really want?"

I asked, "With all the things this city needs and with 40% of the population living below the poverty line, how do you justify receiving a $250,000 tax break?"

He seemed angry at my question and accused me of many things. When he saw that his accusations weren't going to stick, our conversation continued. About an hour into the discussion, I told him about my idea of finishing The Brady Trail. His whole demeanor turned 180 degrees. He was for that, offered help, paid for my meal, but I never heard from him again.

In the end, I never posted the audio and when it came time for the public hearing I spoke about how during 12 hours of budget meetings I never got a sense of long term goals. But I also praised the city for paying off one of the bonds on an enterprise in the city that now has positive cash flow. I never mentioned the fiasco at the first budget meeting and when I sat down the Ward 3 councilman said,

"I have never seen a citizen sit through all the budget hearings. For someone to do that, I at least need to hear what their ideas are." And the mayor seconded.

By Halloween of that year, the Brady Trail was finished and connected all the way to a sidewalk on a major north-south corridor running on the back side of the golf course. Studies done by Aerotropolis Atlanta, a self-taxing community improvement district around the airport, estimated that it would have cost $159,000 to finish the 700 feet of trail that I had been commissioned to do. I built it on a budget of $30,565, a mere 1% of the transportation sales tax revenue that the city receives in one year[40]. Finally, those that lived on the truly suburban west side of the city had a way to safely and efficiently get to downtown, City Hall, the library, the polling place, the MARTA station in ways other than driving a car.

Joginder nursed me back to health (standing with one of his boxing students)

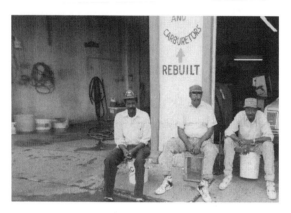

Three gentlemen (all brothers) in Kentucky who helped me fix a flat tire

Epilogue: The Drama of a Changing Landscape at Slow Speed

IN THE SUMMER of 2018, I went back to the area in northwestern Minnesota where the Great Plains ends and the forest around the headwaters of the Mississippi River begins. It had been such an emotional and profound transition for me on that summer bicycle ride that I had to clarify a few things from the journal I had kept.

I felt hypocritical to be driving a car along US Highway 2. I flew standby though and waited for an open seat to get from Atlanta to Minneapolis and then a connection on to Grand Forks, North Dakota. I essentially didn't affect the flight schedule and my ticket, at least from the perspective of the airline, had no value. I have been in airports all day long sometimes waiting for an open seat. So if my flying wasn't carbon neutral, it was at least carbon light.

The airlines are a form of public transportation when you compare the efficiency of airplanes to the efficiency of an automobile with a combustion engine. As big as jet planes are, and as much jet fuel they burn, the comparison might surprise you. Of course it would be more efficient for me to have taken a passenger train or to have ridden my bike. Regardless, these things do matter and know that we are definitely empowered as individuals in facing the challenges of a rapidly warming climate.

It is 1450 road miles from my house to Grand Forks. If I had driven there, I would have burned about 40 gallons of gasoline. Since I would have driven alone, that equates to 40 gallons of fuel per person. But let's say that my wife wanted to see where I had ridden too and jumped in the car with me. Now we are down to 20 gallons of fuel per person. The highest capacity plane going from Atlanta to Minneapolis, a Boeing 757, holds 200 people, not counting the crew. Let us assume it lands in Minneapolis, it lets people off, lets others board, and takes off again for Grand Forks. It is 909 air miles to Minneapolis and 272 air miles on to Grand Forks for a total of 1181 air miles to get to my destination. The Boeing 757 will burn 2,927 gallons of fuel to get there. That equates to about *15* gallons of jet fuel per passenger and a fuel efficiency of nearly 81 miles per gallon per seat. The Boeing 757 was designed in 1982. Fuel efficiency has improved since then and the Boeing 737, designed in 2017, now gets *103* miles per gallon per seat.[41]

Those calculations are for inter-city travel. For *Intra*-city travel, we can compare and contrast using a unit of measurement called "pounds of CO2 per passenger mile," which also takes into account, like the Boeing 737, how many people are riding. In this case however, you want the number to be as low as possible. If I ride the train in New York City, I am contributing 0.15 pound of CO2 for every mile I ride. If I ride the train in Atlanta, I am contributing 0.25 pound of CO2 per mile.[42] The Atlanta train is newer, more efficient, and therefore takes less electricity to run. But the power grid that supplies it gets about a fourth of its power from carbon-free sources while New York City is getting about *half* of its power carbon-free.[43] (Likewise, charging an electric car in Atlanta is different than charging one in New York.) And the average train in New York is about 50% fuller than the average train in Atlanta. For comparison, the average U.S. single (passenger) occupancy vehicle produces 0.96 pound of CO2 for every mile driven. The MARTA bus system produces 0.78 pound of CO2 per passenger mile driven and the average bus is only 21% full. For comparison, the MTA New York City bus system is producing only 0.56 pound of CO2 per passenger mile because the average bus is twice as full (41%). There is a catch-22 vicious cycle at play here; the bus is stuck in traffic because most choose a car, the bus is therefore slow, and so the number of cars on the road increases. Another way to express the catch-22 cycle: Bus ridership is low, the bus system can't justify more buses on the route, wait times increase, people therefore flock to the convenience of ride-hailing, and so bus ridership decreases all the more.

This analysis of transportation choices is only taking into consideration how to reduce greenhouse emissions and stop the upward trend of a rapidly warming climate. When we go into debt for things that seem superficial, we are wasting opportunity to not only improve the infrastructure we need for prevention (e.g. investment into a diverse transportation network) but we are also wasting opportunity to mitigate the impact that a rapidly warming climate will have (e.g. investment into stormwater management, drought tolerance, wildfire prevention, higher tides) from the damage already done. We really have no time to waste. Since transportation and the electric grid are in some ways linked and since both account for more than half of all greenhouse gas emissions in the U.S., investing in a diverse transportation system *and* a carbon-free electric grid at the same time could have a positive multiplier effect. I believe it could be an economic boom and would unite a nation that is currently encumbered by a dysfunctional political system.

So, what bothered me most was the car rental. I rented a car in Grand Forks and turned it in at the Duluth airport so that I could make a one-way trip along Highway 2 and camp and visit the places I had made notations about. I drove 45 miles an hour and turned on my flashers as cars zoomed past me in the passing lane. On the two-lane parts of US 2 in Minnesota, I eased to the 5-foot shoulder that I had ironically used on my bicycle so that cars could easily get on by. This tactic seemed to work well and it allowed me to take in the route about as slowly and safely as possible. I averaged 50 miles to the gallon in a Chevrolet Cruze and used less than 6 gallons of gas to do my research and here is what I found.

I found that some places that I have written about in this book are no longer there. For example, I could not find the bar-and-grill where I had lunch and played the jukebox on the next day after crossing the Red River into Minnesota. Who knows about the rest of the route that I haven't re-visited? I especially worry about those small places in North Dakota and Montana. The U.S. has added 75 million people in the years since and therefore the average density of the country has increased from 67 people per square mile to 86 per square mile. Lakota, North Dakota's, population on the other hand has dropped from 892 to 694. Culbertson, Montana, has gained about one person per year since my ride through there. The café in Fisher, Minnesota, where I ate breakfast on the morning I left Grand Forks and just before I came to the first lake in Minnesota at the town of Erskine, was no longer there. A Cenex gas station on the corner of 4th Street and US 2 was the only retail establishment left.

But I did find the café where I had eaten breakfast the morning I rode to Bemidji, and when I asked the waitress how long the place had been there, she said "since 1991;" I was a patron the year it first opened! Minnesota State Rd 89 merges onto US 2 at the exact location and the lifeblood of a major rural intersection seems to keep the restaurant thriving. I also found the headwaters of the Mississippi River to be as clean and wild as I had found them before. I camped along the shore of Lake Lomond in the Bagley City Park among a grove of birch trees nearby as I had done before, hummed the melancholic lines to *The Bonnie Banks O'Loch Lomond*, and watched the sun set.

References and Notes

(1) Those that live near facilities where recyclables are actually recycled and where the consumer buys product back make a significant contribution to the cause. For example, there is an aluminum recycler about 12 blocks from my home. There is a lot of discussion about this topic but is lacking in scientific research on the intricate math of recycling's effect on net greenhouse gas emissions. The more specific truth is that aluminum is probably the only thing that has enough value to industry to truly spin through the cycle fast enough to make a significant impact on mitigating our consumptive behavior. Things such as glass for example are so heavy to move around and so cheap to make from raw material, the economics of using recycled glass don't mesh with the public's overwhelming desire to re-use it; the carbon footprint from recycling glass is probably greater than it is from just making it from raw material. The largest receiver of our throw away plastic used to be China. So we would ship it to the coast, put it on a ship in probably Los Angeles, and sail it across the Pacific Ocean. China has stopped receiving plastic from the US because the plastic had become so dirty – literally dirty, like with food scraps and such. That tells me that people are using recycling as a means to absolve their habit of over consumption without thinking of ways to reduce first. Even in the bigger picture, I think that recycling now is a way for people to feel good about themselves while making daily choices that adversely impact the planet far worse. How big was that carbon footprint to recycle plastic in China and then have them ship cheap plastic goods back to us that we would toss aside again?

Kimiko de Freytas-Tamura. "Plastics pile up as China Refuses to take the West's Recycling." *New York Times*. Jan 2018.

https://www.nytimes.com/2018/01/11/world/china-recyclables-ban.html

Aluminum Recycling Facts:

http://www.recycling-revolution.com/recycling-facts.html

(2) U.S. Department of the Interior, National Park Service, Glacier National Park http://www.hikinginglacier.com/glacier-national-park-cycling.htm

(3) U.S. Department of Energy, Energy Information Administration:

http://www.eia.gov/petroleum/supply/weekly/

(4) There is an abundance of scientific work published on this topic. Here is just one:

Drake, John M and Blaine D Griffen. Early Warning Signals of Extinction in Deteriorating Environments. *Nature* 467 (2010), 456-459.

(5) Mitchell, John G. "Oil Field or Sanctuary." *National Geographic*. August 2001.

http://ngm.nationalgeographic.com/ngm/data/2001/08/01/html/ft_20010801.3.html

(6) Tax expenditures are those numerous items that we are allowed to deduct from our income. According to many economists and the Simpson Bowles Plan, they should be thrown out of the tax code and Congress should be made to pass legislation making them a government expense that they have to figure out how to pay for. The "zero option" of the Simpson Bowles Plan strips down the tax code and simplifies it while reaching a balanced budget within about a decade. The non-partisan Committee for a Responsible Federal Budget has taken up the advocacy for getting Congress to at least pass a budget and to get deficit spending under control:

http://www.crfb.org/blogs/zero-plan-re-emerges-tax-reform-debate

(7) The Continental Divide that runs through Logan's Pass is better described as the "Western" Continental Divide because there is another Continental Divide in the Eastern US that runs the ridge of the Appalachian Mountains. The Appalachians were formed at a much earlier time in the earth's history and are therefore eroded down to half the height of the Rockies. But height is not the only factor that determines watershed divides - it's also consistency. None-the-less the ridge of the Appalachians, known as the "Eastern" Continental Divide separates a different major ocean, the Atlantic, from the same river system, the Mississippi, as the (Western) Continental Divide does.

(8) (21,596 is half of 43,496):

http://www.ncaa.org/championships/statistics/ncaa-football-attendance

(9) Ayn Rand, Leonard Peikoff, and Peter Schwartz (1989). *The Voice of Reason: Essays in Objectivist Thought*. New American Library.

(10) The following proportional pie chart of US greenhouse gas inventory was created by the author from the listed US Environmental Protection Agency sources below:

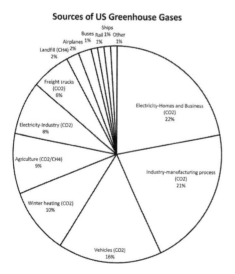

Sources of US Greenhouse Gases

http://www3.epa.gov/climatechange/ghgemissions/sources.html

http://www3.epa.gov/climatechange/ghgemissions/sources/electricity.html

http://www3.epa.gov/climatechange/ghgemissions/sources/industry.html

http://www3.epa.gov/climatechange/ghgemissions/sources/commercialresidential.html

http://www3.epa.gov/climatechange/ghgemissions/sources/agriculture.html

http://www3.epa.gov/climatechange/ghgemissions/sources/transportation.html

https://www3.epa.gov/otaq/climate/documents/420f15032.pdf

(11) McGlade, Christophe and Paul Ekins. The geographical distribution of fossil fuels unused when limiting global warming to 2 °C. *Nature* 517 (Jan 2015), 187-190.

(12) There are many sources of information on planetary atmospheres. Here are two:

University of Calgary:

http://energyeducation.ca/encyclopedia/Greenhouse_effect_on_other_planets

Space.com (online magazine):

https://www.space.com/18067-moon-atmosphere.html

(13) The 2001 Outbreak of Foot and Mouth Disease. National Audit Office (United Kingdom). HC 939 Session 2001-2002: 21 June 2002.

(14) Rannie, William. The 1997 flood event in the Red River basin: Causes, assessment and damages. *Canadian Water Resources Journal* 41(June 2016), 45-55.

Dan Gunderson. "20 years after epic flood, Red River towns no longer dread the spring." Minnesota Public Radio. April 17, 2017.

(15) Okpik, pronounced "ook-pick," is an Inuit word that means "Snowy Owl." There is actually a species of bird we call Snowy Owl (*Bubo scandiacus*). The Inuit are a Native American people who live a sustenance life in the Arctic. They have 50 different words to describe what we call snow, whether it be a wet snow, a dry snow, a blowing snow, and so forth.

(16) Great Lakes Information Network:

https://www.glc.org/glin

US Environmental Protection Agency: Physical Features of the Great Lakes.

https://www.epa.gov/greatlakes/physical-features-great-lakes

(17) Tanner, James T. "Black-capped and Carolina chickadees in the southern Appalachian Mountains." *The Auk* 69 (1952), 407-424.

Brian Davidson, Michael J. Braun, and Brian Scott Davidson. "Cryptic genetic introgression into an Appalachian sky island population of black-capped chickadees." University of Maryland (2011).

(18) US Geological Survey data at Sault St. Marie, Michigan: https://waterdata.usgs.gov/nwis/dv?referred_module=sw&site_no=04127885

(There are 7.5 gallons in one cubic foot of water)

(19) Lake Huron and Lake Michigan are at the same elevation and thus could be considered the same lake. The relatively narrow strip of water at the Straights of Mackinac is the delineation between the two lakes.

(20) United States Department of Agriculture Economics, Statistics, and Market Information System:

http://usda.mannlib.cornell.edu/MannUsda/viewDocumentInfo.do?documentID=1025

Agricultural Marketing Resource Center (production map by locality):

https://www.agmrc.org/commodities-products/fruits/cherries

National Cherry Festival:

https://www.cherryfestival.org/p/about/383

(21) I had an extensive phone interview with a third generation family member of Island View Orchards.

http://maraschinocherries.org/the-growers/island-view-orchards/

(22) Scripps Institute of Oceanography, University of California San Diego:

http://www.oceanscientists.org/index.php/topics/ocean-warming

(23) National Oceanic and Atmospheric Administration, National Centers for Environmental Information, Climate Monitoring:

https://www.ncdc.noaa.gov/sotc/snow/201701

(24) There are numerous scientific articles on the subject of the California drought that lasted for an excruciating 5 years: 2012 – 2017. Here are just two:

Diffenbaugh, Noah S., Daniel L. Swain and Danielle Touma. Anthropogenic warming has increased drought risk in California. *Proceedings of the National Academy of Sciences* 112 (2015), 3931-3936.

Griffin, D. and K. J. Anchukaitis. How unusual is the 2012–2014 California drought? *Geophys. Res. Lett.* 41 (2014), 9017–9023.

(25) Jon Erdman. "Record flooding in April/May 2017 swamps parts of Missouri, Arkansas, Illinois." The Weather Channel. May 5, 2017.

https://weather.com/storms/severe/news/flood-threat-forecast-south-mississippi-valley-april2017

The United States Geological Survey interactive map and monitoring station data:
https://maps.waterdata.usgs.gov/mapper/index.html

(26) Encyclopedia Britannica has a good image of ice age extent:

https://media1.britannica.com/eb-media/18/64918-004-69BCB037.jpg

Shackelton, N.J. Oxygen isotopes, ice volume and sea level. *Quaternary Science Reviews* 6 (1987), 183-190.

Here is a good graphic showing the advancement and retreat of ice that was built from the type of science used in the above article:

https://www.atmos.washington.edu/2001Q1/211/Group_projects/group_D_F00/index.html

(27) Bradley Brooks (Indianapolis Museum of Art). "Athens of the Prairie: How Columbus, Indiana Got Great Architecture." Reason TV:

https://www.youtube.com/watch?v=E8foQ_BC4sU

(28) There are a number of sources for calorie conversions but here are my calculations:

Car:

30,000 = the number of equivalent food calories in one gallon of gasoline

3,200 miles / 30 miles per gallon = 107 gallons

107 gallons X 30,000 calories = **3,210,000** calories of energy burned in a continental car ride

Bicycle:

I estimate that I pedaled on average 10 miles an hour.

3,200 miles / 10 miles an hour = 320 hours of pedaling

650 calories per hour to propel a bicycle at 10 miles an hour X 320 hours = **208,000** calories.

Note: There is a basal metabolic rate (BMR) included in the 650 calories per hour that I would have burned whether I was on the bike or sitting at home on a couch. I have disregarded BMR for simplicity. Subtracting basal metabolism would have lowered the bicycler's required calories to *only* propel the bicycle and would have made the bicycler look even more efficient than a vehicle.

(29) There are about 87,000 commercial flights a day in the US and vehicular traffic emissions are 8 times greater than jet emissions (see reference 12).

https://sos.noaa.gov/datasets/air-traffic/

(30) Raw data from the Mauna Loa Observatory can be found here:

ftp://aftp.cmdl.noaa.gov/products/trends/co2/co2_mm_mlo.txt

Tables and trends can be found here:

https://www.esrl.noaa.gov/gmd/ccgg/trends/index.html

RECENT MONTHLY MEAN CO_2 AT MAUNA LOA

Image provided by NOAA ESRL Global Monitoring Division, Boulder, Colorado, USA

(31) https://climate.nasa.gov/evidence/

Courtesy NASA/JPL-Caltech

(32) Here is one source on seasonal atmospheric CO2 fluctuations:

https://scripps.ucsd.edu/programs/keelingcurve/2013/06/04/why-does-atmospheric-co2-peak-in-may/

(33) Shakun, Jeremy D, et al. Global warming preceded by increasing carbon dioxide concentrations during the last deglaciation. *Nature* 484, 49-54 (April 2012).

The BBC reported on the article in the journal Nature in laymen's terms:

Jonathan Amos. "CO2 Drove End to Last Ice Age." BBC News. April 4, 2012.

https://www.bbc.com/news/science-environment-17611404

(34) For a good description of parts per million see *Skeptical Science*, the non-profit science education organization:

https://www.skepticalscience.com/CO2-trace-gas.htm

(35) For an insightful book on probability:

Mlodinow, Leonard. *The Drunkard's Walk How Randomness Rules Our Lives.* Vintage Books, 2008.

(36) Shantideva. *The Way of the Bodhisattva.*Translated by the Padmakara Translation Group. Shambhala Classics, Distributed by Random House, Inc. Boston. 1997.

(37) Global Issues is a media site edited by Anup Shah. Here is what he says, "My background is a degree in computer science—not exactly a degree in global issues! The point is that you don't need to have qualifications to be concerned and want to do something, although you do need the time to sift through a lot of information to understand what is happening!"

http://www.globalissues.org/article/26/poverty-facts-and-stats

(38) Elise Gould and Hilary Wething. "U.S. Poverty Rates Higher, Safety Net Weaker Than in Peer Countries." Economic Policy Institute. July 24, 2012.

https://www.epi.org/publication/ib339-us-poverty-higher-safety-net-weaker/

(39) Diamond, Jared. *Collapse, How Societies Choose to Fail or Succeed.* Penguin Books, 2005: pp. 494-496.

(40) The tax revenue, known as TSPLOST, is estimated to be $13 million over a five year period for the City of College Park:

http://www.fultoncountyga.gov/tsplost/

(41) Fuel Economy in Aircraft:
https://en.wikipedia.org/wiki/Fuel_economy_in_aircraft
http://www.boeing.com/resources/boeingdotcom/company/about_bca/startup/pdf/historical/757_passenger.pdf
(42) Tina Hodges. "Transportation's role in responding to climate change." U.S. Department of Transportation, Federal Transit Administration. January 2010.
https://www.transit.dot.gov/sites/fta.dot.gov/files/docs/PublicTransportationsRoleInRespondingToClimateChange2010.pdf
(43) Georgia Power portfolio:
https://www.georgiapower.com/company/about-us/facts-and-financials.html
New York power portfolio:
Leslie Kaufman. "How New York is building the renewable energy grid of the future." Inside Climate News. May 25, 2017.
https://insideclimatenews.org/news/24052017/new-york-renewable-energy-electrical-grid-solar-wind-energy-coal-natural-gas

Made in the USA
Columbia, SC
20 December 2018